The Hotel Ione
A Hotel With Spirit

Milly Jones

ISBN 978-1-9393061-5-9

First Print Edition

Printed in the United States of America
Published by 23 House Publishing
SAN 299-8084
www.23house.com

Table of Contents

Chapter 1: Ione, CA, July 1978

The weather was hot, and the light outside was ominously salmon-colored. The swamp cooler and the large fan over the kitchen stove have been left on all night, in an attempt to cool these two rooms. I am sitting farthest from the front door. The door to the hotel lobby is open a few inches it brings cool air in at my back.

One of the regular customers entered. "Morning, Milly. Seen any ghosts lately?"

"Not today; but it is still early."

I was used to being teased about such things. As the owner/operators of Ione's only hotel, my husband Bill, me, our employees and guests have been surprised many times by the antics of a specter.

Mary, an off-duty waitress, sat opposite of me sipping coffee and reading the paper. Two more customers entered and removed their hard hats. They were pushing on one another, so eager to get inside that they left the door open.

"Hey, that's earthquake weather out there!" one man announced.

"If there is such a thing, this must be it," I called out to him. "Nothing to worry about, this hotel is indestructible."

"Shut the darn door, please!" I shouted as yet another man entered without closing it. "You would think that he knew better," I muttered to Mary. "It's bad enough in here already without letting more heat in."

I looked again at the stranger who had just entered. I became aware that there was something different about this last customer. In a town like Ione, which in gold rush days was known as *Bed Bug*, there are all sorts of characters and only a few of them are tourists. This man was old! His white hair stood out in all directions as if he never combed it.

He wore grey cotton pants. The knees were dirty as though he had been working in the garden. His grey woolen shirt had no collar and was buttoned to the chin; strange, on such an airless day. One of the shirt's long sleeves was buttoned at the wrist. The other hung open. He wore no belt.

The man ignored my reference to the door, so one of the other men rose from his chair to close it. The old man shuffled slowly past the first table where another off-duty waitress chatted with a friend. I saw her shiver as he passed her. She looked up at him sharply, but returned to her conversation without comment.

He continued by the second table, apparently intent on reaching either the far end of the counter or the kitchen. One of the customers at that table not only shivered as he passed her, but leaned away from him as if he had a bad smell. I noticed that his shuffling steps made no sound on the linoleum floor. That is when I glanced around at the kitchen where Eva, our cook for that day, stood in the open door to let some cool air flow into the kitchen. She turned to look at me and nodded. Somehow she and I knew this man was not alive. She must have told the waitress on duty behind the counter because the girl remarked laconically, "Oh, Bull!"

This statement was enough to catch the attention of the men eating at the counter, and they turned around to watch the man pass them. No one greeted him. A few of them shrugged their shoulders in an I-don't-know-who-he-is expression, when a buddy asked if anyone knew him.

I stood up suddenly, startling Mary. "Look at this guy!" I whispered to her without taking my eyes off of him.

"Mary, look at this guy, he's dead and no one has told him yet. He should be lying down somewhere!"

Mary's head jerked around; her expression was indescribable as she focused on him. "Oh, God!" she breathed. "I hope you're not going to tell him! Are you?"

"Maybe I'll be embarrassed if he says, 'no, I'm not,' but I've never had such an opportunity before."

I stepped forward to intercept his slow but steady progress. "Hello," I said quietly. "Do you want something? A cup of coffee? The bathroom?"

He was so short that I had to crouch to look directly into his face. He made no sign that he heard or saw me. His unblinking eyes stared through me. As he continued to shuffle, I backed up to stay in front of him, studying him for any signs of life: a smile, a breath, or a glimmer of light in his eyes. There was none.

"Do you want to use the telephone?" I insisted. "Or do you want to rent a room? Are you looking for someone?" He made no response. That was the end of my repertoire of hotel questions. I thought, now what do I do?

"Hey," I spoke loudly, "You're dead!" There – I did it. Every man at the counter turned in our direction. He had walked the entire length of the café, bypassing the counter, and he was definitely heading for the lobby. He would have to cross in front of me to get there.

I noticed that the buttons on his soiled shirt were wooden. I saw that he wore odd shoes, made of some shiny, black material like oil cloth – the kind used for table covering. I found out later that back in the gold rush days, it was customary not to bury folks in real boots, or shoes, because

3

leather was so scarce that it could not be wasted on the dead. These simple slippers were made by the undertaker, if the deceased persons loved one requested it, because it was believed that the dead would not walk the streets of heaven if they were buried with bare feet.

Still determined to confront him, I stood my ground as solidly as I could, not knowing what to expect when he reached me. Would he disappear if I touched him? I was shaking and I began to feel weak.

He made the turn at the table where Mary still sat watching him in horrified fascination. I put my hand out to stop him as he came directly at me, and saw and felt it go right through his shoulder and sink into him. My arm followed. He was made of nothing that I could grasp. He felt neither hot nor cold, but my hand met a soft resistance, as if passing though soft Angora fur. My arm tingled with pins and needles, and the hair on it stirred. So did the hair on my face and neck, as though moved by strong static electricity. I had the revolting impression that he was about to adhere to me like nylon from a hot dryer. If he did, and I had to peel him off of me, I knew I would faint.

He smelled like a wet dog. The fright I felt took my breath away and dried my mouth, but it did nothing to deter his moving forward. Unable to withstand him, I stepped aside against the chairs, and reaching for the doors edge, I swung it wide to let him walk past me into the hotel lobby.

I have regretted that action ever since. Whether it was automatic politeness, on my part, due to respect for the aged, or an instinctive move to clear the way before him so that he would not change course and come at me again, I really cannot say. But if I had not opened the door for him, I'm certain that everyone in the café would have had the chance to witness his walking through solid material before he disappeared

I followed him out through the café door into the lobby, but he faded very quickly, for he was nowhere to be found. As

4

slowly as he was moving, it did seem impossible that he could be hiding somewhere. Eva, Mary and I ran around the staircase and down back the hall, searching the restrooms. While I stepped out of the back entry door they ran for the front door.

I rejoined them in time to hear Eva ask a young man who was standing on the sidewalk, "Did you see an old man come out this door?"

"No," he answered, "no one has come out but you."

"Maybe you saw an old man go into the hotel through the café door about five minutes ago?" I urged him.

"Nope, just two guys wearing hard hats, but they weren't old and no one has come out. I've been here for a half hour."

The sound of thunder rolled over head and large rain drops splattered as they plopped onto Main Street, refreshing the muggy air. Mary, Eva and I returned inside as we speculated on who the old man might be, or might have been. Was this one of the town's former citizens? Had a phantom stage coach stopped in front of the hotel to let a passenger off?

This hotel is a replica of a previous one which burned in the 1890s. Perhaps the room where our café is today was the office where one could register for a room, or sit in front of a potbellied stove, or play cards while waiting for the Sacramento to Jackson stage.

Back in the café, Mary decided to leave. Eva returned to the kitchen, but I couldn't resist asking the customers, "Has anyone seen a ghost lately?"

This brought quite a verbal reaction some of which I cannot repeat.

Maybe he is still in the hotel. If he did stay on, it is fine with me. He was not the first ghost that we were witness to during the year and three months that we had owned The Hotel Ione.

5

Chapter 2: A Pyramid of Smoke

The first ghost that we saw was on June 22. We had the hotel just seventy days. My husband Bill and I had never worked in a hotel, restaurant or saloon, and now we owned all three.

"You have bought yourselves a job," our families said. "How will you manage such a big project?"

We had been looking for a business that would combine our talents and knowledge. Together we felt that we could accomplish this. For moths we had looked at fishing resorts, grocery stores, and motels. We never considered a hotel. Bill, who was working for the University of California in Berkeley, was glancing at the real estate ads and phoned to tell me that the hotel in Ione was for sale. We had visited Ione many times and had admired Preston Castle. It overlooks the town. We drove to Ione, and bought the hotel the next day.

Now we were working harder than we had ever worked before, and tomorrow, June 23, we would be serving breakfast in what we called our "dining room to be." We had been working all morning to remove leftover boxes, tools, cleaning equipment, and assorted junk to make the room presentable for our first Chamber of Commerce breakfast.

I was in the process of moving a few vases of flowers from the café into the dining room in an attempt to relieve the room's stark appearance. The sudden quiet and the dim

6

coolness was an overwhelming relief from the noisy steam-filled kitchen where I had just been.

The room looked as I had left it, except for a charcoal grey pyramid of smoke suspended about nine inches above the floor. It had a rounded top, and its height was taller than my 5-foot 6-inches.

Taking a deep breath I blew at it, breaking it apart, only to have the smoky mass return to its pyramid shape. The skin nerves crept up the back of my neck to the top of my head, where they did a little dance among the hair follicles, then followed a muscle-tightening chill.

I watched in astonishment, while absolutely charged with curiosity, when the smoke began to vibrate slowly like it was trying to express itself. With my heart pounding, I turned away and calmly walked back into the kitchen.

Stacy, a high school senior, was our evening dishwasher. His mother was our evening cook and at this time of the day most of his pearl diving activity was coming from her as she prepared for the dinner hours. He stood with his back against the steel sinks drying his hands. I approached him and whispered.

"Stacy, there's smoke in the dining room!"

He mimicked my words, using the same whispered voice. Then the realization of what he said caused him to run toward the dining room door, still clutching the damp towel. I was right behind him, knowing that I was going to feel foolish. "Where there's smoke, there's fire," didn't apply.

"There's no fire," Stacy said.

"I didn't say there was a fire! Where is all that smoke coming from? Isn't it strange? See how it just hangs there?"

"No," he shrugged. "Not too strange when there has been someone back here smoking!"

"Normal smoke drifts across the room," I explained, as I waved my arms sideways above my head. "It does not stand upright like that. And why is it such a dark color, and still doesn't smell like something is burning?"

Stacy snapped the towel briskly into the smoke. Again it came apart, returning as before to its pyramid shape.

Suddenly the smoke became energized. It vibrated, and then it broke apart into small puffs. We watched in awed silence as it formed a point on its left side, then as if it were behind sucked away by a vacuum cleaner nozzle, it completely disappeared. Stacy stared at me, his eyes wide open in amazement, his mouth sending out a comical scream.

Stumbling into each other in our rush to leave our unusual host, we became momentarily stuck in the kitchen doorway.

"Mom!" Stacy yelled, "There's something strange in the dining room!"

"No, there *was* something strange in the dining room, now it's in here. It's you two," she remarked. "Stacy, get back to work!"

Stacy and I were too excited to do anything except to discuss what we had just experienced. I was particularly thrilled, and I felt ears in my eyes from the wonder of having seen what I truly believed to be a Ghost.

The news of our meeting with a specter traveled fast, and soon the café was filled with the curious. A few of the more adventurous peeked into the dining room. But the smoke was gone.

Chapter 3: The Sexy Lady Ghost

On June 23 the Amador County Chamber of Commerce breakfast went well, with no smoky pyramid attending. The members filed past me smiling and thanking me for such a delicious meal. That made me proud; after all, I did make up the menu.

At 11 a.m. in the café, an extremely long black silk shoe lace, looking like one used to lace up a Victorian lady's high topped shoe, floated down from our newly scrubbed ceiling. At that particular moment, the bartender brought me a curious metal object which she had found on the bar. She explained how it had appeared mysteriously. I recognized it as an axle grease cover, or dust cover from a Model-T Ford.

"Did you see anything, like smoke?" I asked eagerly.

"No," she said emphatically, "and I better not!" She also added, "If I do, I leave!"

I wondered about these simple items – were they gifts from the ghost? I put them under the café counter and said 'thank you' toward the ceiling, not knowing in which direction I should voice my appreciation. My little gathering of employees, I'm sure, were wondering about my stability.

The first week as we were cleaning the café, I found six ruffled pressed glass dishes. I thought that surely the previous owner had forgotten them. When I showed them to her she said, "If you like them, I want you to have them."

"If I like them," I gasped. I couldn't believe my good fortune. I brought my hands together in a praying gesture, and glanced toward the ceiling saying, "Oh God, I'll take a dozen."

Now the stack had grown by one – that was very curious. Maybe one of the employees had one at home. When I asked who had given me the gift of one dish, they all shrugged and gave me that *not me* look.

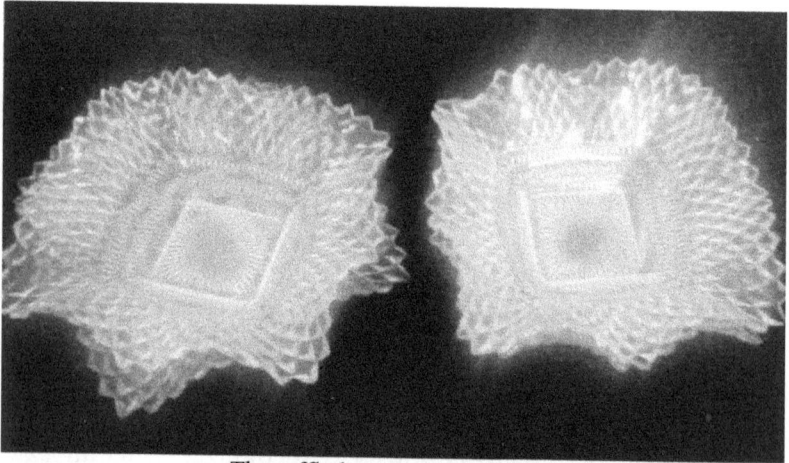

The ruffled pressed glass dishes

I left the café and went to sit on the staircase. It was made of redwood and it was stained with a mahogany color. The sound of the jukebox coming from our very own saloon had a daydreaming effect on me. I recalled the story that the previous owner told to Bill and me. Of how Guesseppi Tonzi had lovingly reconstructed this hotel in the same design as the one which had burned in 1908 – except that the innovative Guesseppi added a glass skylight.

"Good job, fella," I said aloud as the sun streaming in warmed the air around me.

What a cacophony of sounds must have reverberated through the building when this space was open to the elements, when birds, insects and bats were visitors. Not unlike today; yet so different.

Today all the sounds come from the ground floor: voices, music, footsteps, laughter, dishes rattling are channeled up the staircase, to bounce off the glass of the skylight. Then without diffusing, it rushes into each room.

A Room at the Ione Hotel

The hotel was built like the letter H, with two cross pieces. The staircase is in the center of the twenty-one rooms and three baths on the upper floor. Eleven of the rooms opened onto this space, which today could be called an Atrium. The rooms probably looked like they did in the 1930s. All have double beds with old fashioned coil springs, a bureau with a mirror, a bed lamp and a small hand basin.

Not all of these had running water and to our dismay, many times the clogged sink was used as a urinal. There was also a linen room and an office. Most peculiar, the wall along the hallway at room #9 was angled, making the hallway wider but giving that room five walls.

On the ground floor, there were eight doors which also opened onto the Atrium. Of the five on the right-hand side of the lobby, one was the door to the saloon; the others were bedrooms in the first hotel.

Guessepi, by putting the glass cover over the lobby, shut off any fresh air which would normally get into these rooms. There were no outside windows along the hotel's right-hand wall. The walls separating these rooms have been removed; the area became the dance floor and part of the pool table space.

On the opposite side of the lobby were doors to the dining room, the kitchen's back hallway and the café. There was also a door behind the stairs that opened into a bedroom, but this door was kept locked and covered with a drape.

The well to the left of the stairs was made of brick and cement, just a hole in the cement floor covered with a board. Bill's idea to open it and build an old-fashioned looking structure around it seemed right. The well with a wheel, rope and hanging bucket became an added attraction.

The Tonzi family named their hotel *The Golden Star*. This name remained for sixty years, until Dorothy Stacy purchased it and named it the *Stacy Inn*. We thought it was a funny play on words when we renamed it *The Hotel Ione*, pronounced like the city: I-own.

The Victorian architecture of the hotel was an attractive addition to Main Street. Across the front, seven columns stood proudly along the high curb supporting a porch and forming a portico over the sidewalk.

Embossed designs, decorated a row of cement blocks which encircled the building. Standing above the roof line, twenty-six cement, scrolled finials decorated the upper facade. This was topped by four cement urns. The yellow and white colors brought out the hotel's features.

Located forty miles east of Sacramento, its main street being highway 104 , Ione's history says that it was known by several names, two being *Freeze Out* and *Bed Bug*.

One year during the Ione homecoming celebration, a town gathering that lasts four days, Dorothy Stacy thought that it would be amusing to name the old hotel *The Bed Bug Inn* just for the humorous connotation it afforded the hotel. A large bed sheet was painted with the appropriate words and a drawing of a cute costumed Bed Bug named "Benny" designed by Richard Lambert. The sheet was draped from the front balcony and caught the eye of the population. The hotel is still affectionately called *The Bed Bug*, and is mentioned in, *Ripley's Believe It or Not*. Benny is the towns' mascot. Ione has a population of 2,000. Although most of the buildings on one side of Main Street had burned, they were rebuilt in the original old west style.

Besides two alcohol bars and the hotel, there are three restaurants, a pharmacy, beauty shop, two doctors' offices, City Hall, a library, a gift shop, the post office, an automotive store and auto repair, a jewelry store, a bank and a small shopping center.

For the first few months, we rarely had a woman guest. Bill said that I was being silly, insisting that the men and women who shared a room be married. Yes, that is how I felt. It was so strange for me to understand how a woman could lay down with a man she had just met. Also, I was embarrassed for

13

the women. Somehow, I thought everyone would know what she had done. Was she married, was he?

"It is very difficult for me to ask these people if they are married before they can rent a room," Bill said to me. "Rethink this, Milly. We are going to lose a lot of customers if you keep insisting on this rule. You have got to stop judging people by your moral standards. It is making me feel and look ridiculous!"

"Okay, I won't let it bother me anymore," I agreed. "What happens behind closed doors is between two adults; it's their business!"

"Now, that's the way you are going to have to think from now on," he said.

Two of my truck-driving guests reported to me one morning, asking what room we hid that pretty little gal in. I was quick to say, "We don't have any women staying in the hotel."

"The hell you don't! We've seen her twice."

"Really," I answered, trying not to let my thoughts show in my face.

"Yeah," said his buddy. "She puts her finger against her lips, like she is telling us to be quiet, then she walks out the back door."

The other man added to the mystery and gave me a clue that we may have a woman ghost.

"Yeah, she is a sexy little babe. She has a long black skirt and a blouse like a sailor, you know, with a big collar."

"That's a weird outfit; it sound to me like the girl is a bit out of fashion. Did you two follow her? Does she open the door or go through it?"

"We saw her open it, didn't we?"

"Yeah, but I didn't hear it close!" said his buddy.

Chapter 4: George the Ghost

When we purchased the hotel, there were two men living there. The first was Jack, a truck driver, whose family lived in Hayward about a hundred miles away.

The other was Ray Thompson, a seventy-year-old gentleman who had a heart condition. His doctor told him that he must not climb stairs; he lived on the ground floor at the back of the hotel in our only apartment.

Ray could tell the best stories of how he had ridden the train from Jackson to attend high school in Ione. At age eighteen he started work in the Argonaut mine; he told how the men's pant cuffs were inspected for any lingering gold dust.

I liked his tale about the underground baseball games, and how the men would travel on a hand car in the mine. They would flip a coin to decide which town to come into, which tavern or dance hall to visit, after which they would disappear back down into the mines again. He escaped the terrible mine explosion of 1922 which killed many men. This put an end to his deep mining adventures. He went to college and became a pharmacist.

Occasionally Bill found the time to take Ray for a ride which helped to keep him from his bar-stool buddies. These trips were always memorable because of his amazing memory about landmarks. He would tell Bill stories of strip mining and how that process ruined hard rock mining. He seemed to know

15

everyone, never forgetting names; he introduced us to many people.

He was able to take care of himself and his apartment. The only problem he had was that he liked to cook, especially beans. That would have been wonderful if he did not often fall asleep – then what he was cooking would burn. Customers coming into our café were the first to smell Ray's burning food and ask the question, "What are you burning today?"

That would send me rushing to Ray's apartment to turn off the stove and check on his health. His normal place to sit was in an armchair, where he would spend his days reading western pocket books. At night he would come home walking cautiously, having imbibed too much. At such a time, one of us, Bill, I or any of the other regular guests, would attempt to help him navigate the back hallway toward his apartment. He waved his arms in a swimming motion, which somehow seemed to help his balance.

Many times he and I spent a good while as I tried to convince him to let go of the cigarette machine in the lobby. Even though I was sober, I found it difficult to walk with him because I was laughing so hard at the situation.

"Gol-darn-it Milly, there is a long haul ahead of us," he'd say.

"You got that right; do you mean h-a-l-l or h-a-u-l?" I teased.

"No matter how you smell it, it won't be easy," he said.

"Don't you mean spell it?" We laughed so hard at his mistaken words that we both hung onto the cigarette machine for a long time.

"Gol-darn-you, Milly, I hate you," he would say as he chuckled. I knew that this translated meant just the opposite.

The men who lived at the hotel didn't mind the inconvenience of the bathroom down the hall. We did provide a place to sleep, eat, drink, shower and be friendly with people with whom to share their daily experience.

Each morning these men would sleep as long as was possible, before dashing down the stairs to buy coffee, cola, or breakfast. I could tell at a glance who was not present at the counter, and then he would get my special wake up call.

"Mom says it's time to get up," I would say as I pounded on the room door.

Our café enjoyed a constant changing of faces as the men left for their jobs and the later breakfast-eaters took over the tables. The loud chattering grew quiet as our chief of police entered. The newly appointed chief was also occupying a room. Another man, whom I recognized as a guest from Boston, sat down beside the chief and groaned a dull good morning.

"Two coffees?" I asked. "How are you doing? Sleep all right?"

"No," my newest guest answered, "I didn't sleep at all."

The chief glanced around the café casually; he seemed to scrutinize every person. Occasionally, he gave a friendly nod to someone whom he recognized then he reached for my arm to get my attention. He asked in a soft voice, "Milly, do you have an older man about sixty years old, staying up stairs? He has greying hair, medium height, and stocky build. He is wearing a beige zippered windbreaker, white shirt and dark pants."

"No," I said. "I only have one older man and he lives in the lower apartment."

"This man," the police chief gestured to his right, "called the police department last night to report that he was being kept awake by a short old man who kept walking into his room and waking him up. I told him I was renting room #5 and would be home in a few minutes. When I arrived, he was sitting on the stairs, having given up any thought of sleeping."

17

"That's right," the man added. "The little guy was driving me batty. He would walk in to the room and pull on the blankets, shake the bed, and he even pulled on my leg once. He kept saying, 'You can't sleep here.'"

"I told him to get lost and he would leave, as if he were satisfied. Then he would return in a few minutes. He would shake the bed and pull on the blankets, and repeat his message. After the third time, I called the police department."

"The door has a slide bolt, why didn't you lock the door?" I asked.

"Oh that doesn't keep him out," he responded, his voice sounding bewildered.

Bob, sitting to the left of the chief, spoke up. "I heard that description, and it sure sounds like an old buddy of mine." He said this in a let's-tease-the-tourist manner, with a wink. "That does sound like George," he said, leaning forward in his chair as he spoke to the other men along the counter. They nodded a definite 'yes.'

"Which room did you say that was?" Bob asked.

"Room number four," said the tourist.

"That's the room George died in, all right!"

"Are you telling me that I was talking to a ghost?" the tourist asked.

"I don't know, you saw him. You say that he spoke to you?" Bob asked.

"Yes," said the tourist, "I'll never forget it. He sounded like he was talking from the grave. His voice was deep and raspy, like he had a cold."

"Oh, God," Bob said, "I've got goose bumps. That is just how he sounded."

"I'm leaving," said one of the other men. "I don't even want to think about this."

"I'm leaving too," said another.

18

The room began to empty as the men left for work. I felt better when one of them men said, "See you at dinner time, Milly!"

It did cross my mind that perhaps the men wouldn't want to live where someone had checked in, and checked out the hard way, only to stick around complaining about the sleeping arrangements.

I spoke to Bob that very afternoon. "Tell me about your friend – the one who died in room #4."

"His name was George. He stayed in that room while he worked nights at one of the sand plants. He usually arrived back at the hotel about 4 a.m. Many times one of his friends, having had too much to drink earlier in the evening, would remember that George's room was not being used at the moment, and he would then go up the stairs to sleep for a few hours until the owner of the bed came home to wake him up. I guess George still thinks that is his room and continues to wake up those who sleep there. What am I saying – is that possible? I don't believe in ghosts; I was just teasing the tourist!"

Bob took his baseball hat off, and ran his fingers over his hair. He glanced up the stairs for a long moment with a baffled expression on his face. "This is weird!"

Chapter 5: Locking Up the Police

We hired a restaurant management consultant. He showed me how to order food weekly and began our bookkeeping system. We shopped for the right white dishes, glasses and utensils. We bought ten tables for the dining room and thirty antique chairs, and put old fashioned lace curtains on the dining room doors and its only window. We also hung a decorative electric fireplace for atmosphere and installed electric baseboard heating. A very generous friend volunteered for the hardest job, the laying down of the carpet squares in that big room. The only other decorations were my mother and father's wedding picture, my grandparent's picture, my mother's dining room buffet at one end of the room, and a large picture at the far end – a 6-foot x 4-foot photo of a Sacramento River dredge. With gold-colored tablecloths and rust-toned napkins and candle holders, the room took on a cozy and inviting appearance. I felt that there was not a prettier dining room in the county.

I delighted in the thought of our owning this hotel. We had no experience, and little business sense; Bill had never tended bar and I had never been in a restaurant kitchen.

It was silly of us to give up Bill's secure job, sell our home in Walnut Creek and buy a lot of work… so said our doom-and-gloom friends and relatives.

All was going well, except with our restaurant management consultant. We appreciated his work on our behalf, and we felt that he was worth his wage. But he wanted to turn our little café, into a classy, more sophisticated establishment. He changed the waitresses' style of ordering, which meant a new method for the cooks to learn. He required that they also clear their own tables and cut down on their hi-jinx and giggling. I am sure that he was right, however, the spontaneity was gone.

Emmy was our second bartender. She drew her own following, and become a mother figure to many people. If our employees had a problem of any kind, from an illness to a debt, Emmy would always be ready with a shoulder to cry on, or a loan. She was always a good sport.

Emmy is hard to describe, because she seemed to change daily. Her dark eyes had a light in them, a glow that made her happy attitude sparkle.

The third bartender was a redhead named Vicky, whose puffy reddish hair reminded me of Little Orphan Annie, the comic strip character.

Vicky was a happy person and she smiled and giggled all of the time. One day when Vicky was working, our management consultant, who was still trying to help us become successful, noticed that she was not wearing a bra. He mentioned the fact to me, and Vicky explained to us that she had never worn one, and had no money to buy one.

The management consultant then took it upon his self to guess at her size. Probably asking for his wife's assistance, he brought a very pretty brassiere into the saloon.

Vicky did as she was told. She went to the ladies room and she put the brassiere on. When she returned we tried not to laugh. It was impossible. Even the management consultant laughed. She looked like a young child who was trying on her mother's brassiere. The sharp points that protruded from her chest raised the white blouse up in the front and looked obscene. We all agreed that she looked best without one.

We hired our help in several ways. The usual application brought us trained people for the jobs where special training was necessary. Sometimes we used our own method. If they were clean, spoke English, had good manners, and a sense of humor, they could have a job. We were lucky and found a dedication that few employers see in their help.

Our customers were glad to have a familiar face working in the café and we were glad when we could hire Eva as a waitress. She had worked for the previous owner, and most of the customers had known her since she was a child.

This 4-foot 11-inch dynamo, with dark eyes and a pixie haircut, took three steps to everyone else's two. She cheered everyone with her witty personality. She is also remembered for playing a certain prank. This took place before we purchased the hotel, and here is the story as it was told to me.

Ione had at that time two police officers who were very aloof, nattily of their serious attitude. There was an attempt by some to provoke them, but all in a friendly jest.

One morning the former owner, asked Eva to go into the saloon and to open the front door, leaving it open, to rid it of the stale odor of beer and smoke… just as she opened the door to the sidewalk, the two officers walked by. She called to them expressing a secretive look.

"There is someone in the tool room behind the dance floor."

"There is," they whispered in unison.

"It's back here, come on!"

Eva walked on her tiptoes. The officers did the same. She opened the tool room door; the officers stepped inside.

"It must be in there," she whispered, pointing to the closet.

"Step back," one of the officers said, motioning to her. "We'll check it out."

Eva stepped back, right out the door, closing it behind her and locking it with the slide bolt. She raced out of the saloon, returning calmly into the kitchen.

"Guess what I did?" she asked in a sing song voice. "I locked the police department in the tool room."

"You did what, you rascal?" the former owner asked, incredulous at that bit of information.

"Yep, I did, I just locked up two cops!"

"You can't do that; you'll be arrested for false imprisonment!"

"We'll sure miss you if they press charges!" a customer teased.

"They won't press charges!" Eva bragged. "They're not so tough. I knew them before they were police officers, and they won't do anything to me... but they may not laugh."

When she went back into the saloon to free her hostages, the sunlight coming through the doorway blinded her for a moment, even though there was now the dark figure of the police chief filling the opening.

"Have you got two of my men locked in the closet?" he said. His deep voice and commanding presence humiliated Eva.

"Go right now and let them out." He emphasized this order by stamping his foot as if he were chasing a two-year-old.

Eva opened the door and apologized to the men.

"Lucky we had our radio with us," the men said upon seeing the chief.

"And you," one of the officers said to Eva, "we could arrest you for detaining us against our will."

"There has been no harm done," said the chief. "Just a little embarrassment if the story gets out, that's all."

He winked at Eva, a grin playing at the corners of his mouth as the uniformed trio left.

23

Chapter 6: $180, Ghosts & Pickles

It was a very busy three months before Bill or I could consider joining the Ione Merchants Association. Just finding the time to attend a meeting would take some effort. At last one evening, I was the one who went.

While I was away, Bill found the time to do the café register, which only means that he counted the money and had done all of the necessary figuring and paperwork.

When I arrived home from the meeting he told me that there was an unusual problem. We were $100.00 over... one hundred dollars more than the register showed that we had earned.

"Did you collect any rent money today?" Bill asked.

"I sure didn't; you must have added wrong," I told him, although I knew that was unlikely.

I carried the register drawer back into the café, placing it on the lunch counter. I stood with my back toward the register. The old fashioned register was a massive one, black and chrome. To show off its handsomeness, we had it setting on the top of an antique treadle sewing machine which was painted red.

I counted the money as I did every night, and then subtracted any payouts and the amount we started the day with.

"You're right," I told Bill as he came into the café, "we are $100.00 over."

We were baffled. We paid for dairy, beer, wine, and other services, by check on delivery. Our wages were paid weekly. In the beginning, it was sometimes difficult for us to make the hotel payment and the utilities charge when that time arrived. We had money in our personal account, but you shouldn't borrow from yourself to run your business.

Earlier in the day, I had made up the next days' deposit slip and it showed that we would be short $180.00 to cover our expenses unless we earned that much that evening. From our empty saloon? Not likely. I told Bill what my bookkeeping showed.

"We'll make it somehow, honey, don't worry so much." His self-assured grin put my worry at ease.

"It's right here," he said as he tapped the stack of twenties with his finger, "We already have most of it, right?"

I turned to put the drawer back into the register and just like a magic trick had been performed, there were four more twenty-dollar bills.

"Where did these come from? They weren't here a few minutes ago."

"I don't know where they came from, but I will take any more that they want to give us," Bill said, as he gestured with hands, turning to glance around the room. "Gimmie, Gimmie," he joked.

One of our guests came into the café, saying that we had a full saloon, and people were asking for us. He was right – what a surprise! What had been an empty saloon now had all of the business men from the meeting which I had just left.

"We talked it over," Mr. Ding said, "and decided that it was about time that we come in and meet you and Bill!" Someone else added, "Sometimes we Ione citizens are a little slow in our greetings."

25

The next morning when I went to the bank to make the deposit, I looked at the twenty dollar bills in my hand. I noticed that nine of the bills looked different from the others.

I went right to the manager's desk.

"Are these twenty dollar bills good, or are they funny money?" I asked, as I spread them across his desk.

"Where did you get this? How many do you have?" he asked.

"I have nine of them. They came through the register. What's wrong with them? Why do they look so different?"

"They're pre-1920 Silver Certificates, that's why!"

I was glad to deposit them. I have since learned that those nine bills were worth more than face value. So be it! I was already pleased with the amount of the gift. As I passed through the hotel's swinging doors, I remembered to say thanks toward the ceiling.

The following weeks we were disturbed by many unusual occurrences. They were becoming more frequent. Jack, coming home one evening, met a small boy who was standing on the back stairs. These outdoor stairs led to the parking place behind the hotel.

"Hello," Jack said, as he stepped around the child, and continued into the hotel. As the screen door closed, Jack wondered who the boy was. Perhaps his family is staying here.

Thinking that the boy had followed him, Jack turned to see which room the boy would go into.

The boy was still outside looking through the screen. Now the boy had no face. His features were gone, and he was continuing to fade. Jack rushed to the door and swung it open; there was nothing to indicate that the boy had been there. Still shaken when he told this to me, he said, "Honestly, I don't know what made me open the door and look for the boy. I guessed that he was just playing a trick on me! He looked like he was melting and I wanted at least a smudge of him, if not a puddle, left there in his place." I wish that I could have heard the first part of Jack's phone conversation with his wife! It probably went something like, "Hi honey, guess what I saw today!"

In the dining room candles flared or blew out. Chairs were overturned, men had their bottoms pinched and napkins were seen flitting across the room. One evening a fully loaded baked potato with lots of butter, sour cream, chives, and bacon bits, lifted from a woman's dinner plate and dropped into her open purse. A very direct hit.

In the kitchen our apron strings were yanked; sinks filled with soapy water would have the plug pulled out and drained. Gas stove burners that were turned to a low simmer would suddenly become a torch and burn whatever was supposed to be simmering gradually. In other parts of the hotel, balls of light were seen bouncing along the floor of the upper hallway.

One night a guest and her daughter sharing a room were awakened by a short, stout woman who happened to be equipped with her own glowing light. Not a flashlight, but one that surrounded her, as if it were coming from within. They watched in silence, as she attempted to put a blanket on the shelf, which was too high for her to reach.

Thinking it was pretty early for the maid, especially since they were still in bed, the daughter said aloud, "Excuse me, we are still sleeping in here. Could you come back later?"

Without looking at them the woman left. Still clutching the blanket, she walked through a locked door and the light went with her. It became dark, and they had to turn the light on to see that the time was 3 a.m.

One morning I challenged the employees, saying, "Okay, stacks of dishes do not grow by themselves. Someone has donated two more and they are identical to the six that the former owner gave us."

Everyone stared at me, with bewildered expression.

27

"I am grateful, and I do love them, but it would be nice if I knew whom to thank."

All denied contributing to the collection. That is when I moved them into the lower cabinet in the dining room buffet.

Leaving the dining room, I stood in the small hallway between the kitchen and dining room. I was taking a breath of air, and I was drawn to the cool circulating air of the lobby. Stepping through the doorway, I noticed a boy of about nine years old. He was just tall enough to look into the well, if he stood on his tiptoes.

He did look at me, a quick glance, and then he ran under the staircase and around to the other side.

His disturbed look and action, made me wonder if he were one of the disabled children, who attended the local Amador/Calaveras County school.

I called out to him, "Hey, it's all right, you can look into the well. Come back, where did you go?"

Feeling that I was an ogre for frightening him, I went to find him. None of the people in the saloon had a boy with them. The same in the café; no one had seen him. But I had!

He was dressed in a blue shirt with a large collar. The sleeves looked short, as if he were outgrowing it. His hair was a brown color and cut in a Dutch bob, like the child in the *Buster Brown* shoe advertisement. As I thought about him, I do recall one peculiar thing… his feet and legs were fading as he ran.

In the early days of owning the hotel, I was official greeter, gopher (go-for), and all around nuisance. I was able to wash dishes, break lettuce heads apart and wash them, setting them to drain in a large plastic tub. I can follow the recipes for salad dressing, and turn 200 pounds of ground beef into 4-oz patties. I can use the slicer to safely slice onions, pickles, tomato and our newly cooled roast beef.

One morning, I took the last of the dill pickles out of the 5-gallon bucket. I was planning on returning immediately to empty the pickle juice into the sink, so I did not replace the lid securely.

As I mentioned before, no one moved as fast as Eva did. She rushed by me in a hurry to get fresh towels, and she attempted to reach the towel shelf by standing on the pickle bucket. A small cry of, "Oh, my gosh!" made me run into the pantry closet.

There was Eva, standing with both feet in the pickle bucket, juice slopping over onto the floor.

We sent her home to change her clothes. It was very hard to keep from laughing as she left, shoes squeaking.

Chapter 7: Ione Homecoming

The first Saturday in May is "Ione homecoming." If you have ever lived, loved or visited in Ione, this is the weekend that you would want to come home. It is celebrated, with a parade, picnic, horse race, rodeo, and carnival.

Saturday night revelers roam Main Street going from bar to bar, greeting old friends until closing time. Then those who felt the need to party longer would assemble on the street in a noisy mass. Orneriness would take over and someone would do their very best to start a fight. These skirmishes didn't last long and no one got hurt. It seemed to be done in a good-natured way with some, "I'm sorry, Buddy," going on.

As a restaurant and salon owner, we had been told by the other merchants that this would be the one weekend of the year when we could look forward to extra money in our till. Although it was an unbelievable amount of work to co-ordinate and accommodate the great numbers of people who attended this celebration, our first year was made even more frustrating. Unknown to us, the coffee shop across the street closed for the weekend.

We were uncertain as to just how much beer and food to order. Bill was lucky, because the men who delivered the beer knew just what he could expect in beer and wine sales. If the saloon got a beer over-load, it only meant that the next week's order would be smaller. In the café, however, what you order you must use. Fresh meat can be frozen. But what can you do if you order too much salad material, extra milk, or worse, not enough. The words, "I'm sorry we are out of that!" are bad for business.

Our meat delivery day was on Thursday. On Friday, while the crown gathered, we found to our horror that we had forgotten to order the 4-oz steak which we used in our popular steak sandwiches. We checked our three freezers just in case the meat had been misplaced. There were empty spaces in the kitchen freezer where the steaks were always kept in the same spot so that the cooks could grab them quickly. I phoned Craig & Hamilton Meat Co. where we usually ordered out meats. It is located in Stockton, forty miles away.

"This is Milly Jones, at the Ione Hotel. We have forgotten to order seventy-two 4-oz steaks!"

The silence on the other end of the phone line lasted too long, as the woman contemplated how to go about getting this small order to me.

"Milly," she said, "I'm sorry, but there is no one here to cut the meat today, nor anyone who could deliver it. If you can come down here and pick it up, I'll call someone to come in and cut them."

"I can't do that," I said. "This place is a madhouse of activity today. It is Ione Homecoming, and I can't possibly leave the hotel for as long as it would take to drive to Stockton and back. Cancel the order."

I heard her stamp the order. I telephoned Swingle Meat Co., which was only seven miles away.

"This is the hotel in Ione. I want to purchase seventy-two New York steaks."

"I can't do it," the man said. "All the steaks have been ordered already, to be picked up tomorrow."

"I'm the only restaurant in this town; this is homecoming weekend. I know that I don't usually order from you, but I would certainly appreciate it if you could perhaps let me have forty-eight!" I pleaded.

"Wait a minute, I'll take a look and see what is left." I waited almost a minute, and then he said, "I can let you have twenty-four!"

"You are a doll," I said. "I will come right up there."

I happily brought home twenty-four steaks, knowing that they wouldn't last through the day. Wrapped in white butchers wrap they looked insignificant, although they cost a startling sum. During the next three hours, we sold seventeen of them. At 2:30, I counted them in front of the evening cook and waitress, explaining the reason for the steak shortage. I instructed the waitress to print a sign to hang up on the order window as soon as the cook puts the last steak on the bar-b-que. It read: *Sorry, we are out of steak sandwiches.*

It was depressing; I couldn't believe that the next day we would only serve hamburgers. I wished that I could open the freezer and find some steaks. I groaned aloud as I tugged at the door handle, not expecting it to open.

It did, it swung open and we were shocked into silence. Where it had been empty were two boxes of freshly cut, unfrozen steaks. The boxes had Craig and Hamilton Meat Co. on them as usual. The steaks were perfect cut 4-oz. "Wow," I yelled and I hugged the waitress from sheer exuberance, forgetting that I had cancelled the order.

No one delivered them! There was no invoice and we were never asked to pay for them. We did have exactly what we needed. With the twenty-four steaks we bought from Swingle Meat Co. and finding forty-eight steaks in Craig & Hamilton boxes, we had exactly what we needed for the weekend: seventy-two steaks.

Our café had been designed for efficiency in early 1900, but today was out of date. It was a long room with one window and a door that opened onto Main Street. The room was divided in half by color with the upper half an off white color and the lower walls, door, window frames and the narrow cabinets painted a green that we laughingly called mental hospital green. Its flooring was white rubber tile. Five recently installed fluorescent lights which hung from the twelve foot ceiling lighted this cavernous space. A lunch counter accommodated twelve customers; it seated nine along its length and turned to seat three more. The big problem was that it reached the wall. It was a closed end, and the waitresses had to walk all the way back to the other end to get out.

A large heater also hung from the ceiling and a hole in the wall brought in air from a swamp cooler. Narrow shelves and cabinets held all of the utensils necessary for food service.

Although this description makes it sound like an unpleasant room, it had a corny country charm. Like our sleeping rooms, some people did wonder why we did not do some drastic redecorating. We thought we would try re-organization first.

The first thing was to remove the three stools at the end of the counter and open it for easy exit. That left only 9 stools so we added to the number of tables and chairs.

The only decorative molding was a picket fence along the wall by the tables. This made a great place to display antiques for sale. We bought salt and pepper shakers in an old-fashioned style, retained the chrome napkin holders, and placed glass vases with silk flowers on each table and along the counter. The kitchen was the same color green but we were able to paint it off-white. It had a sink that was so low that the bottom was just twenty-two inches from the floor.

Mary, our tallest waitress at six feet, got a backache from bending to wash the dishes. Eva at 4-ft 11-in found it perfect. We had no dishwasher; the kitchen was not set up for one. Around the walls the appliances were placed close together in an effort to make the workings of the kitchen as comfortable as possible. Although we drew many plans, we came up with nothing better.

I wanted to be a cook. How ever there was one big problem – I had no skills for restaurant cooking.

I watched the cook as she handled four pans cooking perfectly fried eggs.

Each night we boiled and chilled twenty pounds of potatoes for morning hash browns that we shredded on order. We sliced ham into 4-oz. slabs; our bacon was special order only, but we prepared large eggs, skinless sausages, and homemade milk gravy for the eighty biscuits we made from our own mix.

The morning cook arrived at 5 a.m., and she had a hard day ahead. First she turned on the oven for the roast beef, then the grill, the steam table and finally lighted the bar-be-que. She then started the soup of the day, and boiled more potatoes for mashed potatoes.

When the waitress arrived she made the coffee, turned on the café lights, unlocked the doors, and then she became the cook's assistant. She made the bin of salad, and went out into the café to greet the first customers.

To understand how fast the cook was, think fifteen people at one table ordering different meals; she could prepare the food and have them all served at the same time. So I watched and I practiced. I ruined food, and I washed dishes.

One morning the cook was sick, so I decided that I would try my new skills. It was a Saturday, no specials today. Vicky our bartender was the first to enter the café.

"Gad-zooks, Vicky what am I going to do!" I admitted to being nervous.

"You don't have a problem Bunkie, you've got me."

Before I could respond, she said "I know how to cook," in a way that led me to the idea that she was a bit intoxicated.

"Why are you here at 5:30 a.m.?" I asked.

"I haven't been to bed yet," she bragged. She put a comrade arm around my neck and led me back into the kitchen, she wrapped an apron around her hips and then she almost disappeared into the deep refrigerator. She filled the kitchen counter with flats of eggs, a tub of butter, and pounds of bacon.

The first orders went well. Hash browns, eggs over easy, and she fried them on the grill. She began to sing the song playing on the radio, which was okay.

The next orders were shaky she started moving a little slower. She became overly friendly; each time someone she knew entered the café, she left the kitchen to greet them.

This was my big chance. The first order was a Spanish omelet – how hard could that be? First, put the hash browns on the grill, next mince green pepper, onion, and cheese. Beat three eggs. Sauté pepper and onion on the grill in a circle, and place ingredients onto the egg and fold up.

"Let me do it," Vicky said, as she came back into the kitchen. "I'm good at omelets!"

I allowed that perhaps I should let her; after all, this would be my first one.

Vicky neglected to cut the cheese into small pieces; it was very cold so it didn't melt. The egg cooked too long and no matter how it was folded it, would not cover the filling. I decorated the plate and filled it with hash brown potatoes, but I knew that the omelet would not be accepted. I was right. The waitress served it.

The recipient looked at it. "Who the hell made this mess?"

"Those two retarded cooks we have working this morning."

"Do I have to eat it? It looked like a battlefield." With the stiff cheese sticks poking through and the green pepper, white onions, and pink ham all showing through the ripped egg covering, he was right.

"Can they make a short stack?" he asked the waitress. I did make a perfect short stack. I also found that I had no trouble flipping eggs in a frying pan. "I'm cooking – yeah!"

For all the goofs we made that morning, the rest of the shift went all right. Vicky was an immeasurable help, and I will always remember her fondly.

"All it takes," she said, "is courage."

I agree, even if it was Dutch courage... which is an expression that means false courage due to intoxication.

When our shift was over, we were painfully exhausted and in our way, we became silly. That is, when I looked at her I decided that, with her puffy red curls, she resembled Little Orphan Annie; all that she needed was two blank ovals for eyes. I cut two slices of cucumber and followed her out to the lobby, inviting her to sit down on the stairs. Then wham, surprise, I laid the cool slices over her eyes. How we laughed. She did look like my comic hero. Cold cucumber may be a new invention for painful, hangover eyes.

Chapter 8: The Staircase Slide

As a child, I had a great time sliding down the grassy slopes of San Francisco's open lands. As summer approached, our neighborhood grocer knew that the local children would be pestering him for cardboard to use as sleds. With a twenty-two tread staircase, I wondered just how fast cardboard would travel over the stair's carpeting. If it worked it would be one heck of a ride. When the new freezer arrived, I quickly took over the packing box; it looked perfect. Because I would have to lie on my stomach, the piece of cardboard would have to be long enough for my body to like full length. I couldn't tell anyone of my plan; no one would understand why at age fifty I would want to do this.

One night, when Bill was across the street at a pool tournament and our saloon and restaurant were closed, I brought my secret carton from the store room. With the box knife, I split the soft cardboard making it flat. I removed my glasses, no use destroying them too, preparing to launch my missile.

"Oh, no!" I said aloud. Someone had walked in through the hotel's front door.

Was it Bill? Or a police officer making his rounds? Either of them might have been able to talk me out of this action. It was a stranger. He gave me a quick glance as he walked past me on his way to the pay phone.

I started thinking to myself that I was losing time! What would this person think about what I was planning to do? I'll wait until he leaves! No I will not, I should have someone nearby, just in case I hurt myself.

I continued my preparation. The man on the phone looked at me curiously as I went under the staircase to take the cushions off the wicker settee. I moved the oak desk from its space at the foot of the stairs, and placed the cushions against the wall where my head would hit.

The man still on the phone was pacing the floor as far as the receiver cord would allow him too, while over his head, I prepared to slide. At that moment someone walked in through the back door. I waited to see who it was. Chris, our nephew and one of our cooks, looked up the stairs to see me with the cardboard and knew just what I was going to try.

"Oh no, Aunt Milly, let me go first," he called, and then he bounded up the stairs.

I relinquished my space at the top of the steep stairs and I watched as Chris spread the cardboard over the top three steps. He had to hold the cardboard to keep it from sliding without him. He kneeled down and crawled forward on his stomach. There was not enough time for him to change his mind. He had only a few seconds to grab the front edge of the cardboard and roll it over his fingers to protect them from rug burns.

Down the stairs he went, like a booster rocket with its launching platform going along for the ride. My heard was in my throat for the time it took him to reach the pillows. As he smacked into them with a great force, I was glad it wasn't me.

He lay there chuckling from the exhilarating thrill and the relief of not being injured.

"Hey are you all right?" it was the man from the phone, and he looked worried.

"Sure I'm fine," Chris answered. "That was one heck of a slide. You want a turn?"

"No thanks," the man said. "I want to live a little longer. Good night!"

The Staircase Slide

At 2 p.m. we who have worked at the top speed for eight hours were naturally still keyed up at the end of the shift. This exuberance, which would soon turn into exhaustion, showed itself sometimes in a childlike manner. If you could escape into the saloon and dance slowly to a restful tune by yourself, the slow exercise would re-energize you.

It was this keyed up zany-ness that made me smear a bright yellow egg yolk down the back of the waitress while she talked on the phone. There she stood perfectly attired, dressed in black slacks, matching the tee shirt and a ruffled taffeta apron. So pretty so sweet and still un-mussed, even after a rough shift.

I had been in the kitchen helping the cook to put the kitchen back into a good workable organization, when I found the unwanted hard-boiled egg yolk. The waitress hung up the phone receiver and faced me.

"You didn't?" she said, as she pulled on her shirt trying to see the back of it.

"I did, I'm sorry, but I'll wash it. I don't know why I did that."

I expected some kind of retaliation, and even welcomed it. Instead the cook laughed and the waitress took after her, first grabbing a fist full of still warm mashed potatoes and a squeeze bottle of mustard.

They ran through the lobby and down the back hall to the parking space behind the hotel, where one of the local young men was refinishing our newly acquired dining room chairs. Down the driveway they ran. The cooks flailing arms and giggling screams, drew the attention of the police officers who were assembled at the end of the drive way. They shook their heads and chuckled, being used to seeing just a couple of the hotel waitresses relaxing.

The cook was cornered against a wall and resigned to her fate, stood still allowing the waitress to rub mashed potatoes on her face and to squirt the mustard striped down each arm.

Coming back into the hotel, the young man remarked as the women walked by, "You look like a corn dog!"

The only problem resulting from this messy experience was that the waitress forgot that she was allergic to potatoes. Her hand blistered in reaction. It is strange, that she couldn't even be around potatoes while they were being peeled. No wonder she was so slim – no French fries!

Chapter 9: Photos on the Stairs

Our hotel enjoyed a steady stream of guests. Most of them were men who worked in the area. They were employed at the nearby sand plants, clay pits and brickyard where Ione bricks have been made for more than 100 years. We also had workers from the Ione Refractory, and the soft coal mine, where a lubricating oil is extracted from the coal. This is only one of the two soft coal mines in the United States; a third is in Germany. Rancho Seco the Atomic energy plant is not in Ione, but in Herald which is fourteen miles away.

The red brick castle, looming over the town, is the old Preston School of Industry, which has been a prison for wayward youth since the late 1800s. It no longer functions as a housing facility. Today the boys are housed in modern buildings, and it is run by the California Youth Authority. There is also a new minimum security prison.

Perhaps eight of the men living at the hotel worked at one of the Ione sand plants. Their boss came into the café each morning to make sure that they were awake and ready to go to work. I kept hearing remarks, unkind ones, about this boss – that he didn't treat the men decently, swearing at them and such. One of these laborers had a bad case of alcoholism. He was like by all his fellow workers and we found him to be a charming man.

He was usually the last man to appear in the café each morning for his eye-opening coffee, and often a beer. The men thought his arrival was right for banter. Their good natured joking and off-the-cuff remarks cheered us all.

"Hey, do you know where you are?" one of the men would ask him.

"I'm on my way to the beach," he would answer, meaning the sand plant.

The boss, who spoke to the men like they were in his custody, was always upset about this late arrival.

One morning after the good natured teasing, he was called to face the boss.

"Kneel down," the boss said as he pointed to the floor. "I don't look up to anyone, especially a slob like you."

The man obeyed, kneeling down as he was told to, on knees that were not too steady.

"Do you want to keep your job, you son of a bitch? You better be ready for work today." While he said this, the boss was hitting the man on the head and shoulders with a rolled up newspaper.

My eyes could not believe what I was watching. I was doubly upset at the other men, because not one of them came to the defense of the groveling figure who being assaulted while his hangover raged. It brought tears to my eyes. I had to do something; I had to.

I reached for the kneeling mans arm, assisting him to stand. Then I twirled the chair the boss sat in.

"You," I said as I pointed to his nose. "Get up and follow me." I had to repeat it; I guess that no one had ever put a demand on this guy. I walked out the front door and onto the sidewalk. As he came through the door, I reach behind him and pulled it closed with a loud slam.

I was shaking from nervousness and anger, the emotional words almost sticking in my throat.

43

"What kind of human being are you? Certainly not one that I have ever seen! No wonder the men speak badly of you. You are a would-be dictator. I don't want you in my café anymore!" I finished by making a cut-off gesture with my hand across my throat.

"You can stay across the street from now on," I added.

"Oh no," he said, shaking his head. "I'm the boss."

He stood with such a sarcastic posture, while pointing at his chest, that I began to wish that he would make a threatening gesture so that I could have given this bum a well-deserved slap.

"If those guys don't get up in the morning, they won't get any work done, and I need them!" He added, "They know that I like them!"

I stared at him and said, "If you called me a son-of-a-bitch, I would guess that you didn't like me. Or maybe I would be called a bitch-of-a-bitch. I'm the boss of this café, and one of the bosses of the hotel, and I will continue to see that they assemble each morning in the café like I usually do, but without you."

He stayed across the street, looking a bit worried, as he watched to see how many men showed up for coffee. Sometimes the men waved to him and sometimes one of them would flatten himself against the wall to make the boss think that he had overslept. I think that they hated to face him each morning! At least now, that could wait until they got to the beach.

We began to notice that a most disturbing odor, smelling like rotting cabbage, filled the air of the lobby on Saturday mornings. We had P.G. & E. check for gas leaks, we had the sewer pipes reamed out, and we spent a lot of money on perfumed spray. We knew it couldn't be a dead animal under the floor, because the lobby had a cement floor.

Every Saturday at 9 a.m. this odor wafted down the staircase. It seemed to turn at the bottom of the stairs and drift down the back hall. Since it would then disappear, we could only assume that it had floated out the back door. We laughed at this saying, "The old lady has gone to the market." It was a signal to tell those of us working that morning the smell was gone. It only lasted for an hour, but it was such a bad smell that we would get Eva to go out to the lobby and spray.

Eva would skip around the lobby as fast as she could, trying not to breathe. Like a fairy spreading fairy dust, she sprayed everything including a man who had just walked out of the men's room.

"Thanks," he said, "I needed that. What the heck is that smell?"

When the man went back into the café, Eva faced the stairs. With her hands on her hips, as if scolding, she shouted at the air.

"I have had enough of your bad smell. I'm tired of having to spray this lobby every Saturday. You are embarrassing me. Why don't you come on a day when I'm not working?"

The following week the smell was not there on Saturday. We were delighted, thinking that perhaps we had gotten rid of it. No such luck; the odor had obliged Eva by coming on Sunday from then on.

Our guests liked the beautiful staircase so much that they wanted to photograph it. That is when we found that we had a startling phenomenon. The photographs taken during the hour that the smell was present did not turn out. Some people braved the odor and stood focusing their camera, not minding it. During the next two years, we warned all who attempted this challenge about the possibility of failure. Many pictures were taken. Most were blank, some completely black, and a few were remarkable.

A woman whose name is Ione, who spends her vacations visiting towns with that name, wrote to tell me that she has four photos which show the banisters and only two stairs in sunlight, with the rest of the stairs looking like a black hole. The next photo has four stairs in sunlight, the next, six stairs, the last eight stairs as the energy mass, specter, spirit or whatever it was moved down the stairs. She told me that she had to request every photo given back to her, whether they turned out or not.

Many people came to challenge the thing on the stairs, to try to get one picture of it, or just to have a weird photo to take home. We had experts, with expensive equipment, and we had simple box cameras. Wonderful electric devices failed to flash, click or produce what they were supposed to, and we heard swear words of differing languages.

One young woman had just arrived in the saloon. She left her husband to order beer while she looked around. When she saw the staircase under the skylight, she just had to have her picture taken. Her husband dutifully went to the car for a camera. The woman ran up the stairs and struck a smiling pose; when the picture came from the camera, she was seen standing in a large cloud-like mass.

"It's a ghost, I know it is!" she squealed in delight. All who saw the picture agreed that it could be nothing else. Unfortunately we do not have a copy of this picture for ourselves.

Chapter 10: The Honeymooners

By 1978, we had ten of those mysterious glass dishes! I have no idea who the generous person was. Oh well, I did say aloud, "I'll take a dozen!" There were quite a few people there to hear me say it. If that person wants me to have their no longer wanted dishes, there is nothing I can do about it! I'm grateful.

I answered the phone one day and I was surprised to hear a woman's voice requesting a room for the weekend.

"My husband and I have planned to spend our honeymoon in old hotels in the gold country, and you are on our itinerary," she said.

"I'm sorry, this is a workman's hotel," I explained. We haven't had a woman guest in a year."

"Ahh…" she said, sounding disappointed.

"These rooms are not like your typical hotel room. They are not beautiful, just clean. The beds still have coiled springs."

"Really?" she asked.

Was that giggle I heard? I continued, "You would have to walk down the hall to the bathroom, and we have no room keys."

"That's okay!"

"The jukebox plays until midnight, and sometimes the men play pool all night!"

"We aren't planning to do much in the way of sleeping, so that won't bother us."

"The cook starts up the kitchen at 5:30 a.m."

"What do you charge for a room?"

"Twenty dollars," I said.

"Oh," she squealed. "That's great!"

I hadn't finished the sentence. At that time we were charging twenty dollars a week.

"If you have a room to rent, we'll take it."

I gave in. Obviously, this woman wanted to stay here.

She said, "That's great, we will arrive late on Saturday evening, so don't give it away!"

As I hung up the phone, my mind whirled. I didn't have a room that I could rent. Why did I say that I did? Standing in the lobby, I glanced up at the room doors, as I recalled to mind each of my renters. An idea jostled my mind.

Room #2 was rented by a man who went home on most weekends I could simply remove his belonging and re-rent the room. Neither the new guests, nor Leo could possibly know. I would have to replace everything in his room before he returned.

When Leo appeared in the café for breakfast, his hair was still wet from the shower. The odor of after shave lotion wafted past me as it was sucked up by the kitchen fan.

"You smell good!" I said in a cooing manner. "Like a man who is going home to his sweetie."

"I haven't decided to go home; in fact, I thought about hanging around here and going fishing."

I stopped immediately – I had to get this guy to go home!

"Now Leo," I said as I walked around the counter and sat next to him. "If you were my husband who had not been home for a week, and was thinking of making it two weeks, I'd be upset. She may have a cozy dinner planned. It's too late to invite her down here to Ione; a woman needs time to plan. Why not consider this. Go home this weekend and take her for a romantic picnic. Then invite her to join you here next weekend to go fishing at Pardee Dam."

"I do have something that I have to do at home," he said. "Now that you have my weekend planned, I would like a short stack and sausages."

"Yes sir," I smiled and I hoped that my feeling of smugness did not show. Back in front of the grill, I sang a little song. Hallelujah!

At 2 p.m. when I was relieved from my kitchen duties, I dashed up the stairs. First to the linen room, then to Leo's room. This room was one which we had decorated. It contained an antique oak bed and a four-drawer chest with a matching maple rocker. A red pot-nelly stove, used as a lamp table, held a lamp that was made from a large, wicker wrapped, kerosene bottle. From our apartment I brought a basket of silk flowers and small bowl and pitcher. The basket fit perfectly in the stove's chimney opening and the bowl and pitcher looked like it belonged on the chest. I sprayed perfume, hoping to disperse the odor of bar-be-que coming directly from the kitchen below this room.

I warned my waitresses, bartender and hotel regulars not to mention anything about ghosts, spirits and such. Also, since they are on their honeymoon I want no knocking on the door or other nonsense.

There were a few smirking remarks about, "How she had the groom, but they could show her who the best man was."

When the Johnsons arrive after 9 p.m., our kitchen was closed. Since they wanted more to eat than the sandwich I was willing to make, they went to Jackson.

The next morning after I had cooked their breakfasts, Mr. Johnson called me out of the kitchen to their table.

"Good morning! How did you sleep?" I asked. I don't usually ask honeymooners how they've slept, but that room is like my back bedroom. "Here," I gestured, "is the second woman to sleep in the hotel since we bought it."

The man grinned and then a warm friendly smile broadened his face. He placed his hands behind his head and said.

"I slept very well; in fact, I died!"

"We don't say that around here," I gasped.

"Evidently my wife had some sort of an experience, though."

"You don't say that on your honeymoon," I teased.

When the pretty blonde woman stopped laughing, she said, "There was another man in our room!" She paused for my reaction.

"What, a threesome? I have got to hear about this."

I drew up a chair. My God, I hoped that Leo hadn't returned.

"The hotel was quiet," she began. "I was awake, but my eyes were closed. As I tried to go back to sleep I felt a presence in the room, like someone watching me. When I opened my eyes, I found out that I was right. At the foot of the bed, stood a short, old man. I saw him because the hall light shone through the transom window. We had discussed hanging a towel over it, but then we decided to try sleeping with the light.

"'This room is taken,' I said. 'You will have to leave.' He just looked at me and although I couldn't see his face clearly, I could tell that he was smiling. I whispered 'I'll have to wake up my husband.' That didn't seem to threaten him. He reached toward the dresser's top and picked up the small pitcher. I watched as he crept stealth-like around the bed to my husband's side, and pretended to pour water on him. all the while he watched me. I was sure that the pitcher was empty, but I reacted by putting my hand over my mouth. If this had happened at home I would have screamed the stars from the sky, but I wasn't afraid! I whispered, 'Out,' pointing at the

50

door. He nodded his head in a bowing gesture and moved backward. I watched the door open; in fact I could see the hallway. When the door closed, I jumped out of bed, turned on the light and reached for the door latch. It was still bolted. So confess – is this place haunted?"

"I have seen a ghost myself, so I guess it is," I answered. "What was this one wearing?"

"Tan jacket, black pants, grey hair. But what do you mean *this* one? How many are there?" she asked.

"We are not sure. Some of our guests have had similar experiences, such as seeing people move about through locked doors. Your description is of a man whom we call George. Until now he has only visited men guests who are sleeping in room four. That was his room nine years ago. Now I don't know what to think; I guess that he must like blondes."

"I told you that he was a ghost!" Mrs. Johnson whispered to her husband.

"Well, I sure do wish that you had shared the experience with me," Mr. Johnson said, his voice sounding as if he had been rebuffed, his lips pouting.

"Honey," she said, as she reached for his hand, "I was afraid that you would have acted rowdy, you know, doing the protective husband thing."

"I couldn't have killed him!" he replied.

We all groaned at that corny pun.

Chapter 11: The Windows and Trees

This lobby is being painted antique gold, with the area around the skylight white for light reflection. The color is wonderful, with dark woodwork.

But what to do with the eight windows surrounding the lobby? Drapes would be out of the question! These windows don't open; if they did, you would see the back of the beer box in the saloon, the dance floor, that card room, into Ray's bedroom and our kitchen sink area. The window at the head of the stair would show our messy linen room. None of them had a pretty view.

Bill's sister, Cedora, a fine artist from Sonoma California, came up with the idea that pleased everyone. She would paint a scene on particle board, cut to fit each window. The window frames became natural picture frames, and the paintings a valuable attraction to the hotel.

The painting of a rushing stream and waterfall went behind the well. One of the glass shelving with knickknacks, and even a sweet-potato vine covered the kitchen window. The two windows hiding our saloon refrigeration had a cute Bambi-like fawn peering from under a bush, and another fairy-like creature among bright flowers. The one that I was fondest of was a white unicorn. His regal pose as he stood among California poppies gave the stairway's landing sophistication.

Painting the saloon would have been a dilemma for the crew who painted the Golden Gate Bridge. Although they would not have to hang precariously several hundred feet above a bay, they would have to contend with twelve-foot ceilings, leftover beams where walls have been removed, water pipes, drain pipes, electrical wires, and a large gas heater.

A load-bearing wall, which ran the full length of the hotel, divided the saloon in two. On one side it was covered with red wallpaper, and was used as a poolroom and dance floor. The room behind the dance floor contained a round card table. One of our bartenders and her husband rented this room and operated a card room. On the front end we enclosed about ten feet, and this space became a small shop with its own entrance opening onto the sidewalk.

This space was rented by Tony. He carried items of interest to children, comic books, popsicles, candy and soft drinks. Also tobacco products. Once when Tony refused to sell a can of snuff to a youngster, the boy's mother came in and purchased the small can and then handed it to her son, saying to Tony, "Do I have to send you a note so that he can have his tobacco?"

"I still wouldn't sell it to him!" Tony answered.

On the bar side, things were better looking, although a bit too modern. Light colored wood paneling covered the walls. Three hanging cabinets separated by mirrors were along the back bar and were lighted by beer advertisements. The bar was twenty feet long.

The saloon was becoming popular with those who drink only beer and wine. Many young men who had come to Ione to attend the fire academy found our saloon a quiet place to spend an evening.

This seemed to bother a certain group of Ione citizens, who just happened to be the same age as the ones they called "the trees" because they wore green uniforms. I heard through the grapevine that our saloon would enjoy a greater crowd if we would keep "the trees" out.

Personally, we decided that we would rather have "the trees" that the ones who were trying to tell us who we should and should not serve. Bill and I enjoyed the company of these men, and become fond of them for the short period of time that they would be in Ione.

We had such a good crowd and we had so much fun that it only took a few weeks for the local standoff to end. Bill and I had never witnessed clannishness before.

One of our bar patrons would pick at the beer bottle labels, littering the bar top with paper chips, which Bill had to clean off.

"If you can remove a label in one piece, I will hang it on the mirror," Bill finally said.

The job accomplished, Bill handed the marker pen to the man saying, "Here, sign it and date it!"

The man wrote, "At last." And a new fad was born. So began our unusual decorations. We were able to confine them to the bar area, along with signs, badges, tee-shirts, hats, business cards and money, which we thumb-tacked to the ceiling. This we donated to Am-Cal.

A problem which began to show itself more each day was that our eight hour shifts were becoming sixteen hours long. As a boss, I was a failure. I couldn't designate jobs to others. It seemed that without even thinking, I had become the only person who could do something right. What conceit! I was working too hard, and becoming teary eyed. Emmy set me straight.

"These people to whom you pay a salary won't hate you if you ask them to do a task. They are here to work, not to be your pals."

Chapter 12: Return to 1910 Days

April 1978... a year has passed since we moved in, and the business is good. We are on the Historic Home Tour this year. We decided to celebrate our anniversary the same day as the tour. Because the hotel first opened in 1910 we called our celebration, "Return to 1910 Days."

We advertised a month in advance, inviting everyone to wear a costume of the era and be ready to play old fashioned games, such as Jacks & Ball and horseshoes. We bought sets of jacks and practiced when time allowed. Patrons of our saloon and Vim's bar found themselves playing jacks. Vim, who was truly a good sport, practiced playing jacks on his bar, getting a laugh and sometimes a challenge from his customers. One night Bill and Pete played a game of jacks and ball in the middle of Main Street. I don't know why they chose that spot, but I would guess; demon bourbon might have suggested it.

Silliness was becoming contagious. A group of burly workmen from the Ione Company of Owen, Illinois challenged the hotel jacks players. The game seemed to be mentioned everywhere. Crossing the street one day two people I didn't know called out to tell me that they had been practicing playing jacks. Could Ione become the jacks capitol of California, like the city of Petaluma is the arm wrestling capitol?

When the day arrived for the party, we were amazed at how many people came to our little celebration.

Busses brought and took away those on the home tour. Some didn't want to leave, saying our open house was the most fun.

We hired a talented group of ten actors from Placerville, California, called "The Apple Hill Gang" as entertainment for the day.

These ten who arrived dressed in old west costumes, miners, cowboys, dance hall girls, a madam, sheriff, preacher/undertaker and one Indian. They mingled with the guests and took turns waiting tables and high hilarity reigned. We were so crowded in the restaurant that our two waitresses had a hard time coping. The actors amused everyone with silly songs and skits and danced the can-can.

The man who was dressed as the sheriff would arrest a cowboy and threaten to hang him. The preacher, hearing these words would reverse his collar, becoming the undertaker. He would then whip out his tape measure and proceed to measure the cowboy for coffin size. The other cowboys would then hustle him away to the front of the hotel, where our balcony made an excellent gallows.

Although the hanging man was safely set up with a harness under his shirt, it did look real. Especially, the way the man was able to twitch his body in realism. One woman who was driving by became so frightened on seeing the crowd and the hanging man that she put up her cars window while her poodle barked a shrill of disgust at our antics.

The car zigzagged as it sped around the corner, its turn, momentarily delayed by the tires scraping the edge of the curb.

The man dressed like the undertaker also played the banjo, constantly playing one tune, *Hang Down Your Head Tom Dooly*. This song drove one of the cowboys to a fury, as he had asked the musician to please, "Refrain from that refrain."

Again the cowboy asked, warning the string-plucker what would happen to him if he should hear that song again. "I'll shoot a hole in that there tummy thumper of yours and hope that I miss the banjo."

When the cowboy walked away into the saloon, the song began again while the musician climbed the stairs. The angry cowboy returned to the lobby. Standing at the foot of the stairs he shouted, "All of you people on the stairs had better move out of the way or suffer the consequences." The cowboy was now a gunman.

The stairway cleared quickly. The banjo player set down the instrument and the gunman pretended to shoot him. The injured man staggered toward the staircase relaxed his body and fell, tumbling down all of the twenty two treads. The crowd applauded this great fall. I must admit to being concerned about the spurs which let scratches on the banisters spindles.

The man playing the part of a Native American was dressed in buckskin, moccasins, and a long black wig. He walked around with a shot-gun, in a broken position, over his shoulder. He was too generous with his time assisting the waitress to serve and order, balancing both his gun and a plate confidently.

Once when forced to walk slowly amongst a line of older women I heard him mutter, "Hmm, me like 'em old and slow."

The dance hall girls waved and smiled at the traffic on the street, while the pretend madam scolded them and pointed back toward the hotel. One of our town police officers had a pretend shoot out with some of the gang. Being the nice guy that he was, he lowered himself to the ground, groaning while holding on to one of the hotel pillars. Bill allowed one cowboy to shoot at his new derby hat and was surprised to find that a pretend bullet had made a large hole in it.

We did have one jacks game, while sitting on the dance floor, sixteen of us. The rules were that when you missed, you were out of the game. Elimination went fast, with much loud kidding. A local young lady won.

Mary, our new waitress, spent her first day working harder than anyone expected. She arrived for work refreshed and smiling. The day was so busy that she worked for ten hours; when she left she was still smiling.

Dominic and Lois Vimini own *Vim's Club*. Orville and Barbara Horst own *Orville's*. Both are alcohol bars.

The *Ozark Kitchen* closed for good when we had been in Ione for a year. The local drive-in was closed when we bought the hotel. We were swamped with customers, so many that we began to serve lunches in the saloon. Bill and I decided to expand the café business and leased the Ozark Kitchen for a year. We hired a new crew to operate that café. How nice it was for us and the customers that two of the *Ozark Kitchen's* waitresses stayed to work with us. We now had twenty-one employees

Since we were the same restaurant, we used the same menu. While the breakfast cook at the hotel worked, I began to work beside her, helping to make double amounts of the soup of the day, mashed potatoes, gravy and the special of the day.

By studying the orders from across the street we learned how much food would be needed there. I would carry that amount of food across the street and put it into the already-heated steam table. We made sure that we had one of our excellent cooks over there that took care of our breakfast and the rest of the lunch menu.

We closed the *Ozark Kitchen* each day at 2 p.m. and kept the hotel café open until 9 p.m. We worked that way for seven months, then our restaurant management consultant told us that he had been looking for a small restaurant and wondered if we would be willing to give up the restaurant across the street.

"Sure we would. It would be great to have friends in our competition." We cancelled our lease on the *Ozark Kitchen* and they acquired it.

Chapter 13: Room #16

One of the strangest occurrences happened very early one morning in room #16. Water seems to be an attraction for these spirits or ghosts or whatever they are, and so far this has been the only real problem.

This room was across the hallway from the bathroom so the man who rented it didn't care that it had no running water. Not only no water, no faucet handles, not even turnoff handles underneath the basin.

Someone reported that there was water running from under the door of room #16. I knocked on the door until the man shouted, "Wait a minute!"

I could hear him moving about, probably pulling on his pants. "Damn, what the hell?" he said as his feet met the wet carpet.

Both of the faucets were running, the basic flowing over. Of course he had not turned them on.

I had to wake up Bill to be shown the right key for the tool room behind the dance floor. I first had to run into the café for the saloon key, cross the dance floor, dash through the card room, unlock the tool room and hope that I grabbed the right wrench.

As I raced back up the stairs I thought of the one thing that I would be sure to today, have two new keys made for my own use. A few more wouldn't matter. I already wore a thin leather cord around my neck, and was teased for appearing like a madam might, with a key to every door, closet, padlock and machine.

The wrench worked. The man helped me to clean up the water, and left. I snooped in the places a spirit might hide and I even felt for cold spots along the walls. I found nothing. How could such a curious thing happen?

My grandmother once told me, "There will be many things in your life that you will not be able to explain."

That room full of wet carpet is one of them; the other is why I remember homilies. I thought that I ignored her when I was a kid.

Chapter 14: The Man with the Gun

A new female bartender's first night on the job is usually a busy one. She attracts the eligible, and those who are not eligible but are interested in seeing a new pretty face and figure. I expected this new young lady to be able to hold the attention of the group who regularly visited the saloon each night.

Instead she came to me in the kitchen and told me that she had a situation which she could not handle.

"There is a man in the saloon with a gun," she said.

I followed her into the saloon, not at all surprised to find there was only one customer at the bar… and he had a gun.

"Hi," I said. "I'm Milly, who are you?"

I thought that if I learned his name, perhaps I could write it in blood just in case he should shoot me.

He ignored me, as he continued to sip white wine.

"Are you okay?" I asked. Again, he didn't answer, but instead stared straight ahead out the front door, not even acknowledging that I was speaking to him. I studied this short man. I hoped that I wouldn't be asked for a complete description. He had a severe military haircut and manner. His well-cared-for facial skin and his manicured nails might have caused me to think that this was a bright and intelligent man.

Looking into his eyes I saw that his outward appearance belied the strange personality within. They had a smart but cruel look in them, like on television on the wildlife programs when you see the eyes of a coyote watching a rabbit. I became the rabbit, as he backed away, in order to have a long view of me. Then he spoke in a pleasant and personable way. His soft voice eased my fright.

"Yes," he said. "I'm okay, are you okay?"

"I'm not okay about your gun," I said, trying to keep my voice as soft as his was. "I do wish that you would put it back into your pocket; you are frightening the young lady."

"She looks neither young, nor frightened," he responded.

Swell, I thought; what am I going to do now?

I asked my newest employee to follow me out to the lobby phone where I hoped to find police intervention. When I told the woman who answered the phone at the police department my problem, who I was, and where I was located, she connected me with an officer. Here are the answers I gave to his questions.

"Yes, it's a small gun!"

"Silver blue!"

"I don't know if it's loaded!"

"I don't know if he's drunk!"

"No, I don't know his name!"

"No, I've never seen him before!"

"Yes, you bet we served him, we'll give him anything he wants!"

"What does he look like?" I repeated in amazement. "He is short, maybe fifty, blonde crew cut hair. I really have not looked for any tattoos, sir."

"Great, you say an officer is on the way? The officer on duty is Miss Victoria!"

I hung up the phones receiver and spoke to my bartender. "Believe me, it is not usually like this, and you do not have to go back into the saloon with me. Go and sit in the café until the man is removed"

When I entered the saloon once more she was walking right behind me. He was still sitting in the same spot, sipping wine, gun on the bar.

As Victoria, our only local woman officer, walked in I nodded toward our only customer. She approached him cordially.

"Hello, are you from around here?"

"Not too far away!" he answered.

"What is your name?"

He told her his name and continued to explain his presence in a rather sarcastic monotone of a voice, as if it were absolutely none of her business, and the only reason for telling her was to placate a probable rebel of the Ione police force.

"I am waiting here for my sons to come from the high school. My car is right outside. I am sipping this wine, not drinking that heavily, and when they arrive I will leave. You got that?"

"I got that," the officer said. "Is the gun loaded?"

"Sure it's loaded, I have a license to carry it, and that is all that's necessary, right?"

"Not really, you must also have a stable character."

He laughed without looking at her and said in a reflective way, rather than a joking manner, "Are you saying, that I'm acting like a horse's ass?"

"If the horseshoe fits," she grinned.

He smiled at her and put the gun into a pocket.

"I am going to make my rounds," Victoria said. "I'll be right back."

I walked with her through the front door. I could not believe that she was going to leave.

"Just do not antagonize him!" she whispered. "There is a backup officer on his way."

"Why not wait until he arrives?" I asked.

64

"He has put the gun away," she said, "and I think the situation is now under control. He is calm. Stay out here until I come back."

Bev, the bartender, standing behind me asked, "Where the hell is she going?"

"She assumes that the man is no threat, as long as he keeps the gun in his pocket."

"Doesn't that make it a concealed weapon?"

"It seems that way to me," I answered, "but she is the officer."

We stood side by side in the saloon's doorway, hoping to ward off any customers from our gun-toting patron.

People had begun to line up along the curb. They must have heard about our dilemma and they were hoping for a show.

We heard a loud voice behind us, our gunman, saying, "I hate cops, especially women cops. If she comes back in here, I will blow her away."

I grimaced at that remark. The treat made a serious situation much more serious. If he was trying to upset us, he was doing a good job.

He certainly was upsetting me. My customers were gone. My bartender was afraid to continue to work here. My compassion for people less fortunate that myself was waning fast. I really wanted to walk up behind him and smack him on the head with a pool cue. No, that is also considered a deadly weapon. He was feeling good with his little game working so well, causing all of this fuss. With my luck, he would come back next week.

We watched, as our only hope of rescue was sauntering along the sidewalk checking doors that were already locked for the night. Where was her backup? No one was in turmoil except me! As if out of the atmosphere, four teenage boys appeared. They clowned and shoved each other rushing past us, filling the saloon doorway. Bev and I relinquished the opening rather than be crushed in the squeeze.

"Hey old man!" one of the boys called.

"Oh, my God, don't talk to him," I said, reaching for one of the boy's shirts. I was sure, that I was saving them from danger. Maybe this guy hated teenagers more than he hates lady cops.

"He has a gun in his pocket," I whispered into the boys back.

"Have you been threatening these nice ladies with your gun? You dumb old bastard, that is going to get you into trouble. Someday, someone is going to believe that you mean it and shoot first."

"Oh yeah, what do you know. I want you to give me fifty, right now!"

"Now, dad?" the boy whined. "Here on this floor?"

"You want to do seventy five?" the man asked.

"I guess not!"

The gunman smiled, satisfied, that his orders would be obeyed.

The boy fell immediately to the floor and started the requested pushups, while the others dutifully counted.

"Do them one handed, you piker, you shirker; your brother can do them with no straining."

The boy jumped up. "Enough, let's move it, we can't stay here all night soothing you military ego, we have home work to do!"

The gunman gave the boys a shy smile and a shrug.

As the group of boys surrounded him and guided him out of the saloon, I saw another officer standing in the lobby doorway.

The boys left hurriedly, climbing into the car at the curb. With one of the boys driving, they left. Our lady officer and our newly arrived male officer met to stand with me, while the bartender went back to work.

"I'm not sorry to see him go," I said.

Everyone who was standing patiently on the opposite curb converged on the saloon to find out the gossip.

"What took you so long to get here?" I asked our male officer.

"I've been here for quite a while, you just didn't see me."

The evening turned financially successful for us, due to the story being related form person to person. Bev stayed to become a fine bartender. The man with a gun? I heard that he has received some mental help.

Chapter 15: Room #4 Revisited

Two of the men living in the hotel were brothers who had
returned for several years, staying three months each time. We
were fond of them and were glad to have them visit. One of
them was under twenty-one so everyone treated him as a
younger brother.

One day the boys received a message to return home. The
younger brother left while his brother stayed in Ione. We
moved his things into the older brother's room and we
promptly rented the now-empty room.

When he returned un-announced, the only room we had
vacant was #4, since that room was now considered to be
haunted, we had begun to rent it regularly to guests who were
interested in experiencing the phenomenon. We decided to let
him use it until another room became available; he agreed. By
the end of the second day, he had already gotten into trouble by
being rude to a waitress. He complained about the food, which
he had always enjoyed, and began drinking heavily. We were
bewildered.

His brother told us that he had turned twenty-one while
away, but he had no answers to the sudden behavior changes.
We became concerned when he stopped showering and grew a
week's beard. He had turned into a slob. We told him that if he
were depressed about something we would be glad to listen to

any problems he might be having. Perhaps we could offer some advice. I wondered if the spirit in #4 was disturbing him.

We now had another room empty. We told the young man which one and expected to hear that he had moved out of room #4 to the other room. All remained quiet. When the older brother came into the café I asked what the reason was for the delay.

"I would like the housekeeper to clean that room before she leaves today," I pleaded.

"He says that he doesn't want to move!" the brother said.

Bill, I and the brother knocked on the door of room #4.

"Time to move," Bill said in a cheery way.

"I don't want to move," the young man grumbled.

"You'll have to if they want you to!" his brother said.

"Seen anything of the ghost?" I asked. The question was certainly worth a try.

"Sure," he readily admitted. "He and I are buddies, he doesn't bother me. I like him!"

"That's it," Bill said. We all gave an agreeable nod. His brother and Bill surrounded him and rushed him out of the room. I followed with as much of his belonging as I could carry. Then we locked the door of room #4.

That was scary. We thought of never renting it again. The young man returned to his normal sweet self within thirty-six hours. Maybe our imaginations were working overtime; I have no other answers. Also, still no answers on where these mysterious dishes are coming from. We have eleven. Oh well I did say, "I'll take a dozen."

Chapter 16: Napkins on the Stairs

Our dining room had been reserved for a luncheon, hosted by the Amador County Police and Sheriff's Departments. Mary was the lone waitress. In the café the lunch crowd had dwindled, giving Eva a lull in her busy waitressing duties. Thinking of Mary working alone, Eva went into the dining room offering assistance with the table clearing.

Eva got right to work. Finding that two of the reservations had not been used, Eva picked up the two salads which were free of dressing. They were pulled from her hands and dumped on the floor. When everything she reached for became a spill or tumble, she understood that she was being teased by something that she could not see.

There were still four officers deep in conversation, and they looked at Eva with a mixture of concern and humor.

"Are you all right?" one of them asked her.

"I guess that I am more tired than I realized."

Motioning to Mary to follow her out to the lobby so that she might explain, in private, that she thought that a spirit was playing tricks on her.

"I will probably just keep making a mess; I'm sorry. I had better go back into the café."

Returning to the café and stepping back into the routine of waitressing, she picked up an empty place from the counter intending to place it into the dirty dish tray. Once again, an invisible hand took the plate and threw it on the floor. The customers jumped, startled at the sudden loud sound. Naturally, Eva became very upset and embarrassed. She certainly was not a careless, accident-prone waitress.

Because her 6 a.m. to 2 p.m. shift was almost over, Eva asked if she might leave early.

"Yes," I agreed, "And to please take the mysterious imp with you when you do."

The Hotel Ione Lobby

She suddenly realized that she had forgotten to get some napkins from storage. Because we had no room in our pantry

71

for such a big box, the napkin supply was kept in the linen room upstairs.

When Jude our evening waitress arrived, I told her about the strange events of the past half hour. That gave us the same thought – Eva could be very vulnerable on the stairs.

"You don't have to watch me, that makes me feel stupid!" she called to us as we stood below in the kitchen doorway.

When she started down the stairs, she was carrying five bundles of napkins. Each of them was a 300-count size and had a glued band around them. When she had reached the 4th step the bundles flew up into the air, as if some bratty child had punched them from underneath. They dropped like large snowflakes, littering the staircase.

Judy and I rushed to her aid. When she stopped screaming she sat on the stairs and cried in frustration and fright. Bill and his customers appeared in the saloons doorway.

"What happened?" he asked, worried about our safety.

"I'm not hurt," Eva told us when she recovered from the shock. "But I'm glad it doesn't pick on me every day."

I was shocked but very relieved to see that she didn't write *I quit* on her timecard.

Chapter 17: Meeting the Medium

Each table in the dining room has a candle in a deep glass container on it. At night, we check them with the overhead lights turned off to make sure none of them have been left burning. For two consecutive mornings, we have found one burning on the same table. The one nearest the spot where I had seen the smoky pyramid. We started removing them from the dining room and placing them in the kitchen on a metal table.

The candle problem, the smoky pyramid and Eva's trouble on the staircase made one of our breakfast guests ask for more details. As I explained the happenings and awful odors to her, she smiled an in a pleasant way she said, "It sounds as if you have a spirit. Sometimes they can become kind of rough and cause all kinds of trouble. They can disturb your guests, but maybe I can help. I mean, that I could try to get rid of it."

She told me that she would be glad to hold a séance in the dining room where I saw the first spirit.

"We can try spirit writing!" she said.

I wasn't too sure what spirit writing was, or how we would go about trying it.

"All you would have to do is assemble a few participants and choose the night."

I was apprehensive. "At night? Why does it have to be done at night, because it's spookier?"

"It would seem so," she answered. "Actually your body slows down at night, which makes you more receptive, and besides, it's quieter."

"So you've done this before?"

"Yes, I have. I'm Rachel."

As I sat opposite her, I studied her and found that she was very pretty. Her light brown hair had a natural curl that I would have liked to have been blessed with. She had an intelligent look and conversation, not kooky at all; just quiet and sedate.

I have no problem believing in spirits, but I have been a skeptic about mediums. I really didn't want to get involved. If I didn't believe, why should I lead this woman on? My mind whirled; could her family sue us if she didn't wake up from the trance? Would she charge for the service of a medium? Could we get our money back if the spirit didn't leave?

"I wouldn't charge you anything!" she said. I must admit to being amazed; did she read my mind?

"If the spirit activity gets worse, give me a call." She scribbled her phone number on a napkin and pushed it toward me.

"Let's be serious, it's a puff of smoke. It can't do a thing without human assistance. I'm not worried."

We stood up as she prepared to leave. She gave me a pat on the shoulder, which I felt was a you-poor-unsuspecting-and-naïve-person kind of touch.

Then she said the most disturbing thing. "The awful odor you smell in the lobby is the spirit. Sometimes the dead bring the smell of death back from the grave. Goodbye, call me if you need me." She walked away and out the front door. For me to accept this new theory concerning the presence of spirits was going to take a major attitude adjustment.

It seemed to me as though the hotel's atmosphere had changed. Now I felt like I being watched. As if the spirits knew, for the first time, that I understood about them.

I would have to speak to Bill about holding a séance. I knew that he would think it was all baloney. What if Rachel is right and our guests are bothered by those spirits, like Eva was? That wouldn't be good for business.

The lobby was empty as I crossed it heading for the saloon to speak to Bill, but now I could tell that the spirit was at the foot of the stairs, or in the vicinity, because of the scent of a bad embalming job.

Chapter 18: Dogs, Bats, and Donkeys

Animals and hotels do not go together. Public health and good sense both play a part in the strict rules. Some four-legged creatures did entertain us in the saloon, and a few were able to infiltrate our watchful system and were found up stairs.

One of the local men had a dog who would sit on a bar stool and take a lunch of jerky from her master's hand. Tammy the dog seemed to smile a *thank you* when prompted to do so. One of our residents brought in a donkey who would also sit on a bar stool. It would eat anything. Where he kept the donkey, I have no idea.

Tommy's miniature dachshund, when set atop of the pool table, could push every ball into the pockets. The dog would look over the side of the table to see if any had fallen to the floor. When the table was cleared of balls, he would run to the end of the table, which had the money slot, and beg for more money to be put in. His wining plea and whipping tail could bring a few coins from customers.

Upstairs most of our guests made the mistake of opening their room's window. Although the hotel had air conditioning and thermostat heat, it was never the right temperature.

One young man opened his room's only window at the top and bottom. Unknown to us, the old wooden window screen was warped in such a manner that the wide opening at the top of the screen became as attraction for thirty fruit bats.

The young man in the bed yawned and stretched beneath the sheet, happy that the alarm clock had not yet heralded 5 a.m. As he moved his feet one way, something moved the other way; many little feet scrambled on top of him. He turned on the lamp to find the horror of nightmares: a quivering blanket of fuzzy bats covering the top of him. He stared in disbelief, momentarily afraid to move. Then with a great thrust he flung the sheet back covering the bats.

He raced from his room and into the one next door. Bursting in, he vaulted over the bed's foot rail stomping all over his buddy. Dan, terrified from being so roughly awakened, jumped from the bed with his fists up, ready to fight. The light from the hall was all that Dan needed to see the crouching figure of his friend pressed in fear, against the wall. •

Switching on the overhead light, Dan yelled, "Jesus H. Christ, what's wrong? I can be dangerous when I'm scared, but now I'm too scared to be dangerous. Did you see one of Milly's ghosts?"

"Bats, lots of bats!"

"Bats, where?" he asked, looking around. "You must have had a bad dream. Beer and chili will do that to you."

"I wasn't dreaming, go see for yourself! They are all over the bed!"

Dan went to look for the alleged bats. When he came back, he stood in the doorway laughing.

"Damn you, Mark, you got me good. I should bend your skull! There is nothing in your room, no bats, no elephants, no little, blue men!"

"The hell there isn't – maybe they flew out the door!"

Both men went to the other room.

"See, there are no bats in here!"

"They are under the sheet," Mark said and pointed.

The alarm clock sounded. Its shrill sound was enough to startle the dozing bats. Their agitation was enough to convince the men that the bats were indeed still under cover. Dan removed the sheet. The bats moved closer together, indignant at the sudden bright light.

"Yuck, they are ugly!" Dan examined them closer. "They look like fruit bats; they only eat fruit and insects. I know you're not an insect, I'm not so sure about the other. They'll spend the day hanging from the bed springs and this evening they will go out the same way they came in."

Still uneasy, Mark grabbed his clothes, boots and hard hat. A new day had begun. As the story was retold, you can bet that every screen was checked.

I didn't appreciate the new weekend guest taking his bicycle apart to work on it while he sat at the top of the staircase. I did look at him to see if the chain was greasy; I said nothing.

Judy came over and asked if I knew about the gigantic dog that was upstairs in room #3.

Bill knocked on the room's door. "I'm sorry," he called. "You will have to leave your dog our in your truck. We can't allow dogs in the hotel."

The door was rudely jerked open and the man faced Bill. "Oh yeah? Well who let you in here, you old goat?" the man said.

Bill was so shocked by this rude person that he asked me to phone the police. The officer who came, although he wasn't on duty, was our chief of police. He dressed like any of our local ranchers would while rounding up cattle, in denim jacket, jeans and flannel shirt, hat and cowboy boots decorated with horse manure.

Armed with the renter's check, the chief bounded up the stairs secure in thought that, this would be settle with just a few words from him. No one answered his first cautious knock. The second knock was loud and demanding, and the door opened suddenly.

"Well what do you want?"

"I'm here to ask you to leave. Here is your check."

"Another goat, this place is full of goats," the man scoffed, referring to the beard that, like Bill, the chief also wore.

"Send someone bigger and with more authority."

The door slammed again. The chief could hear the man speaking to someone.

"What a joke! You should see who is acting the part of an old stage driver. He has on a great costume!"

The chief knocked once more. Again the door opened quickly.

"Okay, let's deal with this," said the room guest.

"Here is your check, sir. You are to take this, and leave quietly. There are not two people with more authority than Bill and I! He owns the hotel, and I just try to impress upon people like you that rudeness won't get you anything in this town, of which, I am the Chief of Police."

"Prove it!"

The chief pulled his jacket aside, feeling a bit embarrassed that his badge was hidden.

"I'll be damned," the rude man said as he grabbed the check. "We'll leave, give us half an hour. Actually, my dog's house is better than this room."

I had been watching from the stair landing. When he noticed me he said, "I hope this business fails; that you have nothing but trouble." He put up two fingers in a V for victory sign. Then peering between his fingers, he said, "I hope this place burns down."

I don't think that his curse worked, unless a curse can take nine years.

Chapter 19: The Ghost Photo

One Sunday morning a college student came from Sacramento. He said that he attended either Sac State or Davis College; I do not remember which. He came to visit the hotel at least once a month during the summer and he was fascinated with trying to photograph our spirit phenomenon on the staircase. He arrived one Sunday bringing a young couple with him. He told me that color film for his Polaroid had become expensive, but he had purchased a package of black and white film.

The trio proceeded to take pictures of each other posing on the stairs. As I watched the first photos develop, I mentioned the fact that this was the first day of day light savings time. Our clocks had been turned back an hour. The spirit should walk down the stairs between eight and nine.

"It is only 8:45, so maybe you'll be lucky today!" I said.

"Take my picture anyway," he said as he placed his long-legged body halfway up the stairway.

When the picture developed we were shocked to see that he was not alone in the picture. A woman whom we could not see with our eyes had shown up in the photo. She had her right arm around the young man as if she were posing with an old friend. She wore a blouse with a low scooped neckline, and she had a lot of dark curly hair. We could see the stairs through her image. With a great yell, we all jumped around and hugged each other.

"I heard of a newspaper offering $50,000 for a photograph of a ghost, this is surely the winner!" he said as he danced around while holding the photo aloft.

"Can I hold it?" I asked. It was really a picture of a ghost. I finally had the answer to a baffling mystery.

"I must make a phone call," the young man said. "I have a friend who owns a photography store, and maybe he could enlarge this!"

While he was on the phone, I took the picture into the café. This was certainly too exciting to keep among such a small group. I wanted to shout it. I wanted everyone to see. I was deliriously happy, to have proof of one ghost.

The usual Sunday morning breakfast crowd took my blockbuster news with the same excitement as I felt. I showed everyone who had heard the stories which I had been repeating for a year. The police officer shook his head in bewilderment. Patty, an off-duty waitress and her daughters and Jan, our breakfast cook, expressed the same wonderment.

The young man put the photo into his shirt pocket as I told him of a money-making idea.

"If you could have the picture made into a poster, I would be glad to sell them for you here at the hotel."

I never heard from him again. I can't remember his name and I haven't heard any news of the photo.

Chapter 20: The Séance

Our town librarian had arranged for a group of historians from De Anza College to visit Ione, reserving our dining room for a special dinner. The hotel looked great! We had added fresh plants to our lobby and the menu was exceptional. With two cooks and two waitresses working, we were more than ready.

Although the dining room sparkled, I was nervous. There was no smoky apparition, but there was a bad odor. It was the now familiar odor of the spirit. Spirit or not, I had to get rid of that smell. I couldn't count on it to drift away before the guests arrived.

I remembered that someone had given us a gift of a Pyrex jar containing shaved wax and a wick. The patchouli and lavender scent of the candle was so overpowering while not burning that we never used it. I lit it and set it on the antique buffet, letting it burn for fifteen minutes before blowing it out and pinching the wick. The guests began to arrive so I put the candle on the top of the buffet, pushing it back on the shelf out of sight.

The next morning, when I came down the stairs, the whole hotel smelled like patchouli oil. I rushed into the dining room to find the jar with the candle had been brought down and left burning on the service top. A metal disk and a teaspoon of wax remained.

Was the spirit trying to contact us, as Rachel had told me? I can't have candles burning at the whim of a spirit. The first hotel had burned down; if our insurance heard about this they would surely raise the premium. If I could prevent a fire by holding a séance, I was all for it. Yet another part of my mind told me that this was goofy thinking and I was not in favor of holding a séance. This became a turmoil in my mind. When I wasn't busy I was thinking about the possible consequences from a restless candle-lighting pest. If it could light candles, could it also start a fire somewhere else? I talked myself into holding the séance and I made the phone call to Rachel the medium.

It was arranged for Saturday night at 10 o'clock. Four of us, myself, Judy, Chris, and Rachel, met in the dining room. With only one candle glowing, the usually bright room took on an eerie atmosphere. I felt that we should have someone attend this séance who was not connected to the hotel as an employee.

"I shall go and find someone," I told the rest, and went out to the street, where I met a young man on his way home.

"Hi, Randy, will you help me with something?" I asked nicely.

"Sure," he answered. "You want something moved?"

"Not this time," I answered. "Come with me."

When I brought him into the room's darkness he hesitated, but we soon convinced him to join us.

"Why does it have to be this dark?" I asked of our medium. "If we write anything, how will we read it?"

"It isn't necessary for it to be dark, just dim. We aren't setting a mood, we are quieting your nerves, and at the same time intensifying your senses."

We began the séance by holding hands and praying for God to protect us.

"From what?" I asked.

"Because we have no way of knowing if this is a bad spirit, we ask for God's protection. It might hit you on the head, or cause some other unpleasant rowdiness."

As we waited for something spectacular to happen, my reserve of bravery melted like wax from the can. Each of us had only a few pieces of paper, ripped from a writing tablet, and a pen which we were told to hold in our normal writing position, with relaxed fingers.

Rachel spoke into the dimness, "We know you're here. Who are you?"

All was quiet; no one moved. Rachel whispered, "If anyone feels their pen moving let me know!"

"Sure," I answered, although I was still unconvinced.

I glanced at each face around the table. They were all so serious that I felt embarrassed. I would have to get serious also.

Rachel pounded on the table. We all jumped, and then simultaneously as if connected to one another, there was a collective sigh of relief followed by a nervous chuckle.

"You had better answer me," Rachel's voice demanded. Gosh, I though. What could Rachel do if the spirit didn't answer? I wouldn't threaten if I were asking questions. I think this thing has the upper hand. We started with a prayer and now she is threatening?

Rachel spoke again. "Are you a man or a woman? You have given us reason to believe that you have a problem, and we are here to help you solve it. This is Milly Jones." Rachel touched my shoulder as if she were introducing me to an old friend. "She owns the hotel now and you are disturbing her and her guests."

My feelings changed. An introduction to the dimly lit room upset me. Was the smoky pyramid standing near the table, peering into my face? At that moment I was not keen on this event. For the first time, I felt scared enough to cry. Now I was serious.

My forearm began to feel strange; it ached and felt full and heavy. The pen began to write with no help from me. My hand felt out of control, like when I was a child having my first writing experience. The letters, large and crudely-shaped, spelled *woman*. I could not put the pen down; it stuck to my hand alive with static electricity. When the pen finished writing the word, it suddenly released and dropped to the table.

"Woman," I read aloud. "That didn't hurt."

I eagerly picked up the pen, leaning it against my hand in writing readiness.

"What is your name?" Rachel asked.

She repeated the question. My pen began to write I glanced around the table, to see if anyone else was writing. They weren't, but I could see in the dimness that they were ready for the moment when and if something moved their hands.

Again my hand moved. The pen dropped when the words were finished. I held the paper near the lighted candles glow. I could barely read it.

"Mary Phelps!"

"Thank you, Mary Phelps." Rachel said. We all repeated this polite action.

"Tell us Mary, what is wrong? Why are you here, and what do you want?"

Wall on fire my hand wrote.

"Were you in the fire?"

Yes.

"Did you die in the fire?"

No.

"Who died in the fire?"

One Child.

"What was the child's name?"

Jon Phelps.

"What was the date of the fire?" I asked.

85

Would Mary answer me? I had no way to get the answers to the questions which I thought were important unless I could ask them. There was a long pause, as if she were making a decision about me, while I brazenly took on the role of medium.

My hand wrote either *1884* or *1894* and I would later use both dates in my research. My hand continued to move drawing a square and the words: *bathing sink no water.*

Now I asked the tricky question, "Which room had the fire?" this was a trick question, because not only is this another hotel, I know that the rooms numbers were removed and the plan reorganized. Also this hotel did not exist until 1910. I also knew that the previous hotel did not burn down until the 1990s.

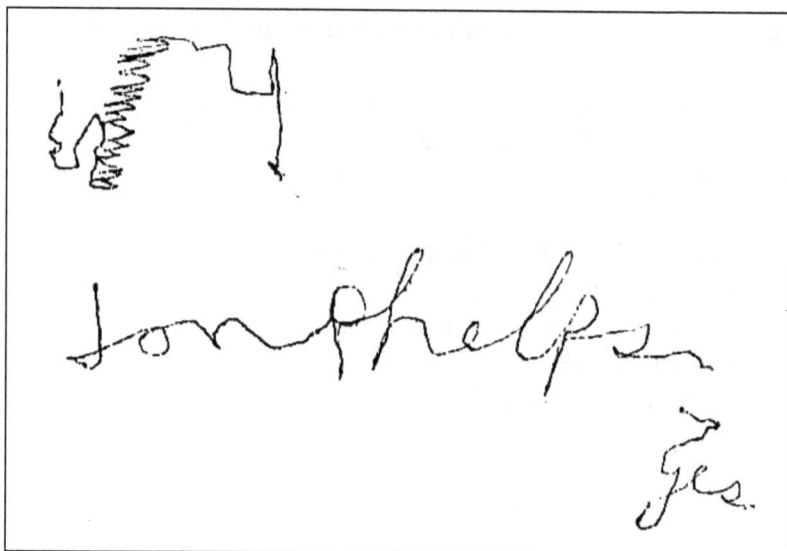

The Automatic Writing: Jon Phelps

The pen drew lines in an ascending design, then one line continued at a sharp angle, zigzagged and stopped. I scrutinized the sketch by the dim light of the red candle in the jar. I was baffled.

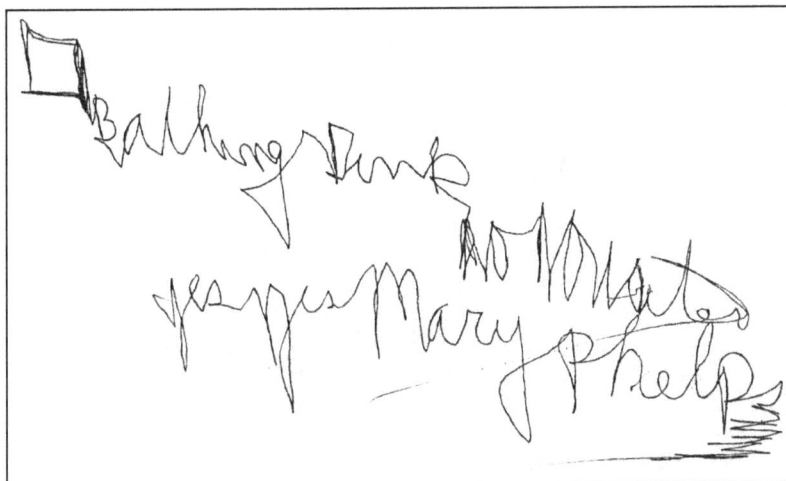

The Automatic Writing: "Bathing sink no water" and "Mary Phelps"

"Pick up your pen, I want to try something," Rachel whispered.

"Be more specific, Mary," Rachel coaxed.

Now I felt sad. How could we help this poor woman? Certainly not by teasing her with questions that she couldn't answer.

My pen began to write a sentence. I spread the papers to accommodate the words: *Go where the wall is bent.*

The pen stopped clinging to my hand and the fullness left my arm.

"This is fun! Imagine talking to someone who is no longer alive. I'm not even nervous. But I don't know where the wall is bent."

The next day, we took the spirit writing papers to the café's counter, where I could always find an answer to any question. I handed the papers to the local citizens, asking if any of them knew of a family named Phelps.

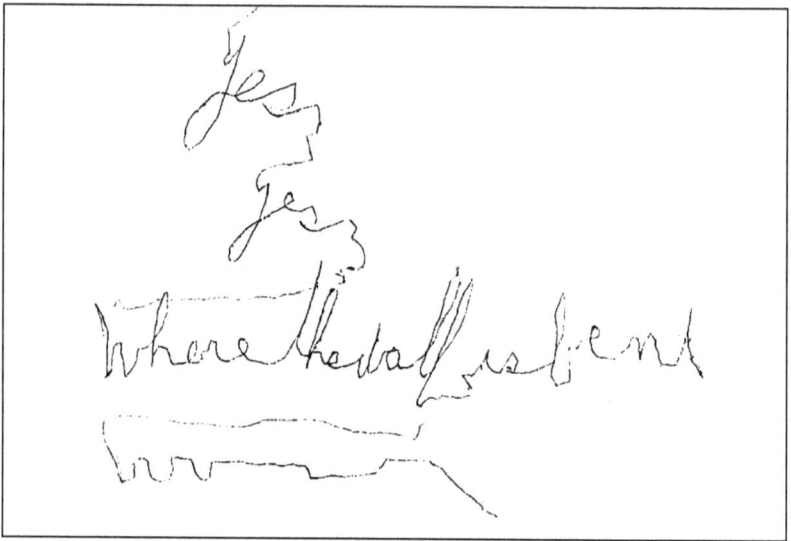

The Automatic Writing: "Where the wall is bent"

One person volunteered. "I remember a family with that name! Ask Evelyn Angers, she's the town's librarian and historian. Also ask Mrs. Bishop; she was born in Ione and her father was one of the town settlers."

Emmy was about to start her bartending duties and had come in for the saloon key, which we kept on the café register. I showed her the spirit papers and ask, "Emmy, where in the hotel is the wall bent?"

"The wall is bent in the upper hallway! Doesn't it curve outside of room #9?"

"You're right, room #9 has five walls!"

The lines that Mary had drawn back and forth in an ascending design was a drawing of the staircase. Its lines also told us to turn to the right at the top of the stairs. She is a clever woman who genuinely wanted us to know about her. She couldn't know the number, but because this hotel is the same design as the last one, she remembered the rooms' direction and where the wall bends.

First I went to the library, for the books of Amador County history, then to the archives, the newspapers morgue, and even the phone book. The information we were able to decipher didn't tell us much.

Rachel, our medium, explained that Mary must be caught in a dimension between life and the world where she should be resting.

I knew that I would do all that I could to find out how to help Mary, but I am a mortal, a living being subject to death. Mary is already dead. According to *Webster's Dictionary: A spirit is a disembodied soul. The human soul; the mortal part of man as distinguished from the body which it occupies.* The body without a soul is dead. Now Mary can be spoken of in different terms, a supernatural being, a spirit, a ghost or an apparition. Every spare minute that I can find, I would study.

On Christmas day Bill, Ray and I were invited for dinner at the home of a local family. There were five children there, and Ray, who loved children, was looking forward to his visit. I had seen him early in the morning, as he came in to ask me for the third time, "What time are we leaving today?"

"We will knock on your door at 1 o'clock."

At the appointed time I went to visit with him to see if he had his shoes on. Sometimes he removed them while he napped. My usual way was to enter his apartment, cross the kitchen and knock on his sitting/bedroom door while averting my eyes from its small window. When I knocked and got no answer I looked in. He was asleep in his chair; a pocket western open on his chest, and his mouth open.

I went in and spoke to him. He didn't answer. I felt for a pulse at his cold wrist and listened for his breathing, then tapped on his chest hoping that I was wrong. I sat on the low stool by his chair, and put my hand over his and I spoke to him for the last time.

"Ray, we love and we will always be glad that we had a chance to know you."

I went to tell Bill that our friend had died, and to phone the police station. The officer arrived to confirm my observation and put up a yellow streamer. An hour later the funeral parlor's transportation arrived. A sad Christmas day.

Chapter 21: The Civil War Ghost

A group of people had reserved rooms for the weekend. They joined into the hotel's camaraderie, and asked me to tell them the ghost stories. One non-believer made jokes of my stories and found great fun in teasing his friends. He stole the sheets from the bed in room #2, hiding them in the bureau drawer of room #6.

Before they could retire, the sheets had to be found. To great hilarity, they put the sheets over their heads and paraded around the lobby, calling on George's spirit to join them.

Up the stairs they marched, still hidden by the sheets.

"Where are you George? Come out, come out, wherever you are." They repeated this phrase in a sing-song chant.

The sheets were hung over the banister to wait until they decided that the party was over, at which time they would have to remake their beds.

The women have convinced themselves that perhaps a specter was hiding in the bathroom. They put on a silly act about accomplishing that task, picking a partner which was often their husband. The rest of the group stood in the hall assembled for a final good night, good luck and a few so-longs, just in case they didn't make it through the night. It was such fun pretending that a ghost might possibly appear.

"Don't forget about George," one of the women said.

"Good night George," everyone said in unison. Then it happened. As if someone had turned on a light, there stood a small man. White hair, tan jacket and dark pants. His body, like a picture on the air, added within seconds of its appearance. The screams lasted longer than the spirit did.

This experience unnerved everyone, and they went to their rooms quickly. I felt bad that the sight of our friend George put such a bad feeling on their party.

One who was no longer doubtful about the spirits was the prankster. Since he didn't believe in such things, and was not at all sleepy, he and his woman sat on the staircase. They were seated there a few minutes lounging and enjoying the quiet. The back door at the end of the upper hallway opened – this is the door which let down the back stairs to the parking spaces.

I was going into my bedroom when I heard the heavy footsteps. I was unseen by the couple on the stairs as I looked to see who was coming into the hotel from that direction. The woman snuggled against the man for comfort.

Along the hall the footsteps came nearer. A civil war soldier, in blue uniform, came into view walking slowly down the hall. He jingled and he rattled as he waked, because of the authentic trappings that he wore. Hanging from his person was a sword, black powder rifle, powder horn and canteen. A ring of keys, clinking together sounding like ghostly chains, added a chilling fear to the imaginings of the couple on the staircase.

The soldier vanished into the darkness at the opposite end of the hallway. I of course was glad to see that Brian had gotten home safely from a bivouac. He was a member of company C, an organization that performs Civil War skirmishes for entertainment.

The couple on the stairs, believing that they had seen a ghost, jumped up and quickly went into their room.

The next morning the group assembled for breakfast, all except for the two who had seen Brian arrive home. I told them about the ghost that their friends had seen, explaining the whole funny story to them.

They laughed and found the experience hilarious, promising never to tell the couple that the Civil War soldier was a man in a costume.

When the late-for-breakfast couple did finally join the others, telling about their experience, their friends responded with, "See, we told you that this place was haunted!"

Chapter 22: Mary Phelps' Family

Thursday through Sunday, we opened the dining room and served dinners from a different and much fancier menu that we had been using in our café. Cooking from two menus would have given the Great Chefs of New York a headache. For me, during the four hours when I cooked hamburgers and fries for café customers I also made apple stuffed pork chops, or scampi in wine sauce and frittata for the dining room. It became unbelievably chaotic at times, and more than once brought frustrating tears. At those times, having a dependable waitress to assist me when she could was essential.

Lucky for me, with Judy working from 2 p.m. to 10 p.m. on Saturday night I smiled through our tough evening duties. After 5 p.m. when the dining room opened she not only had to continue to take orders and serve the café, but she would run the entire length of the hotel to serve in the dining room. She would dash to the bar for a wine order, and then back to the kitchen to dish up soup for the dining room. After she delivered it she would help me decorate the dinner plates, prepare the dining room salads, remove the soup bowls and serve the salads. Finally she would write the checks for café food, collect money, and go to the register to make change.

She would run back to the dining room carrying four of the large, 11"x13" platters fully loaded with food. She still had to take desserts, coffee, handy-wipe packets, the check, mints and running the length of the hotel, return with change and take home cartons for leftover food. When the guests left it was also her job to clear and reset the table, and if she had any spare time, she could always wash the dishes.

Judy was pretty and slim. Her waist-length black hair hung in a ponytail. She wore a costume in keeping with our Victorian theme – a long black skirt and a white ruffled blouse. I wanted the waitresses to be comfortable, at least their feet, so we asked them to wear black oxfords.

The shoes were not glamorous, and the girls laughed at them calling them their 'nun shoes.' In happy defiance, Judy wore cowboy boots.

"Whew!" she said, as she stopped to rest with her back against the refrigerator.

"Are you okay?" I asked, becoming worried about her.

"Do you have a short handled broom?" she asked.

"No, I don't think so, why do you ask. Did you break something?"

She opened her eyes wide, then with a humorous grin she said, "No, I want to shove it up my ass, then I also can sweep the floor as I go about my duties!"

We laughed and I hugged her, realizing that I wasn't the one with the hardest job.

Tomorrow we would talk to Bill about getting another waitress for the café during the hours that the dining room was open. Also, I realized that we should give Judy a cash drawer for the dining room.

At 10:15, the cleanup man got there. He mopped the café and the kitchen floor each night, just as Judy has served dessert and coffee, and collected payment for dinner.

"I'm ready to leave," Judy said. "If they want more coffee, will you serve it? They want to talk to you, they loved the food."

"I am not opposed to taking a bow for a job well done," I boasted, as I followed her into the dining room.

"Here is the cook," she announced.

I was tired and silly, and expecting to see familiar-faced Ione citizens, I took a hold of my soiled apron, lifted it and curtsied.

"Applaud the chef," someone said.

These people were strangers; I had embarrassed myself.

One of the young ladies said, "I love the hotel. We didn't know that Ione had a hotel, or such a terrific restaurant."

"When we drove down the street we noticed that there were two restaurants, both open late. The one across the street is Mexican, and we felt as cooks go we could not be surpassed in that regard. "We," she gestured, around the table, "have written a cookbook on Mexican cuisine. We are glad that we came in here, and we will be back. Judy told us that this is a workman's hotel and that you have twelve permanent guests."

"Yes, they are all men!"

"Except for those who float in and out," Judy remarked.

The men laughed at that. I didn't want them to think that the hotel attracted ladies of the evening, so I added, "She's talking about the ghosts."

"You have ghosts? What fun, I love ghost stories. Do you know who any of them are?" one woman asked.

That seemed to me to be a strange question – to suppose that the haunted could possibly know the name of the specter.

"Sure," I answered, being nonchalant about the question. "The man who haunts room #4 resembles a man named George, who lived here once upon a time. We have found our through spirit writing that the smoky apparition I saw here in the dining room is a woman named Mary Phelps."

There was sudden intake of air around the table, as if all eight of them, had a great shock. One man had stood up.

96

"I'm going into the bar; I don't want to hear this." Even before the woman spoke, somehow, I knew that I had found Mary's family.

"Okay, tell me what the shock was about," I said.

The young lady looked at me with a stunned expression. "My great-Grandmother was named Mary Phelps. So was my Grandmother. My mother uses Phelps as a middle name, as do I."

I began relating to them all that had happened. I showed them the spirit writing papers. Judy was so fascinated, by the coincidence that she stayed and we all talked until midnight.

"What about a child named Jon, who died in a fire?" I asked.

"I don't think that Jon is a name that our family used. I'll ask my grandmother; she will know."

The next day the young woman returned, bringing a well-kept genealogy book. In it we found a page that explained about the death of Ian Phelps, who died in Ione City in 1884 when his room caught fire.

Most of the spirit occurrences were so short in duration that we could hardly recognize them as such. It was only after pondering on the strangeness of what had just happened that we would decide if it were caused by human hand, or one of our unseen friends.

One of these occurred when my sister, Pauline came to visit. We entertained her by talking her into playing pool, a game which she had never attempted. We kidded her about beginners luck and told her she was a pigeon – someone whom we could play against and win easily.

Bill is a good pool played, and he gave her instructions on the proper way to hold the cue stick, and how to rest her left hand on the table making a bridge for the stick to slide over, on its way to strike the ball.

Then the strangest thing happened. She became a professional, making only the most daring and fantastic shots. We watched as the ball did a sharp left turn, instead of hitting her opponent's ball. She also made perfect bank shots and one ball leaped over another instead of striking it.

She won her first game of pool. And loves to tell the story about how the spirits just wanted to help her win. Someone definitely did!

Chapter 23: The Lady in Red

Occasionally we hired a band. This gave us a small financial boost, even after paying the musicians. Those who wanted liquor for their refreshment would walk from one establishment to another, and then return to the hotel to dance.

One Friday evening when our saloon was busy and the music was loud, a middle aged couple walked in. While the man ordered two bottles of beer, the woman glanced around at the dancers and she said, "What the f--- is goin' on, you got a party or somethin'?"

Those words brought silence and cold stares from those within hearing. Emmy placed the beer in front of the couple and said, "Bad language is not welcome in here!"

"Oh, did I use bad language?" the woman said as she leaned against the bar. "I'm a truck driver, and you know how it is with us truck drivers!"

"Not the ones I know," Emmy said as she collected the money from the man and walked away.

A long string of bad language and a quarrelsome voice brought Emmy back, just as I approached the woman from the customer side of the bar.

"Whoops, did I swear again?"

"Yes, you did," I said.

"I'm sorry again," she muttered, as she looked me over disapprovingly.

I looked at her escort; he was very intoxicated and ready for sleep.

"Hi, I'm Milly, and I own this place," I said as I offered my hand. She didn't move, but the man took my hand and gave it a weak shake.

"Do you know this is a hotel?" I asked, as I gestured toward the lobby. "We have a vacancy! Would you and the lady like to freshen up, maybe lie down for a while?"

"Yes ma'am, I sure would!" he answered without hesitation.

He followed me up the stairs and as I opened the door, he rushed past me and actually fell upon the bed and began to snore. I could not believe how fast he had gone to sleep. It was lucky that I had gotten him out of the saloon, and luckier that he was not still driving the truck.

I went back into the saloon where I found his woman drinking from both bottles of beer.

"He's asleep already," I said as I approached her. "That poor guy was tired!"

"Poor guy, shit, he's an asshole. He didn't have to drive this far. Where the hell are we, anyways? We could have stayed in Stockton. They got more bars there, and they don't care how you talk."

"Icks-nay-own-e-stay," I called in Pig Latin to Emmy.

"Sticks and stones."

I repeated as she approached, "Consider the source."

"Will you follow me please?" I asked the woman. "I want to show you where you friend is." She hesitated long enough for me to look at her. It seems that lately I am describing people like cartoon characters. This one was very thin and could have been Popeye's girlfriend Olive Oyl. Her red two-piece pant suit clashed harshly with her orange hair. She teetered on high heeled wedge sole shoes; her eye liner color of blue grey was smudged giving her face a hollow look, while two red spots highlighted her cheek bones.

When we were in the lobby I said, "I am offering you a free room for the night. We often do this for truck drivers. It's a kind of rest stop," I lied. "I'll bet your man is lonely and wondering when you are coming to bed. He is quite a hunk," I lied again. "Why don't you go up there and love him?" What am I doing, I asked myself as I waited for this intoxicated person to move. I have gone in a year's time from not wanting unmarried people to share a room, to trying to force that arrangement on this couple. Oh well, anything to preserve the peace in the saloon.

"How did you find out he was a hunk? Did you feel him? Maybe you got yourself a little screw while you were showing him the room!" she grinned and tipped her head.

Her remarks angered me. What rudeness! Controlling my composure, I said, in my most motherly voice, "You are here only because of my good nature. I will not put up with your insults. I am trying to do you a favor. I hope that you will stay here and accept the room as a gift. If you decide not to stay, our police officers will soon notice that you are a stranger in this town, and un-escorted. You might find yourself spending the night in the county jail's drunk tank."

She sighed, and holding onto the newel post at the bottom of the stairs, she removed her shoes. This made her pants too long to navigate the stairs successfully, and she constantly stumbled. When I opened the room door for her, she glanced inside at the sleeping man and laughed, saying, "Well, look at the party pooper."

Her weaving gait, made her reach out and grab onto the bed. I didn't wait to hear if he responded, I closed the door wishing that I could lock it on the outside. I hoped that these two wouldn't multiply in the dark, as I momentarily listened for any re-occurrence of the quarrel.

I walked to our apartment, where Bill was resting. I told him that I had just rented – for free – room #15 to a couple who are very drunk.

"I sure hope that they go to sleep and don't cause any trouble. He man is okay; he is sleeping," I explained, "but the woman is a weirdo!"

"Better in the hotel, I guess, than on the road." Bill said, giving an exasperated shrug.

A sudden loud crash startled us. We ran down the hall trying to distinguish where the sound had come from. We walked around the stairwell and watched as the saloon patrons came out into the lobby to gaze wonderingly up the stairs, and asked, "What happened?"

"We don't know!"

Approaching room #15, we heard a strange thumping sound coming from within.

"Maybe she jumped on him and the bed broke," I teased.

Bill said, "Oh no, that room has an iron bed; it's not going to break."

Bill pounded on the door. The sound was a demand to open the door.

"What the f--- do you want?" the woman's voice asked. Bill tried the door; it was unlocked, but he found it hard to push.

"Don't you come in here!" the woman screeched.

"Oh, yes I will!"

We soon discovered that the wash basin that hung to the left of the door was now on the floor holding the door shut. It took the strength of both of us to open it so that Bill's arm would fit through the opening and rumble the iron basin, with its drain pipe still attached, out of the way.

The scene in the room was of a woman in a very peculiar predicament. Like a bird with one wing, she was scooting along the linoleum-covered floor, doing a butt hop, trying to get away from us. Her behind was stuck deep into the metal waste basket, where the little finger on her right hand was wedged in tightly along the side of her buns.

It was obvious that she had attempted to use the hanging basin for a toilet. She had balanced on the basin's edge, putting all of her weight on the old wall screws. The basin tilted and she slid off plunking down into the perfect sized opening.

She had ignored the sign above the basin which read: *Do not use this basin. The bathroom is down the hall to the right.*

I put my hand on the angry woman's shoulder saying, "You need help."

I was able to pull her out while Bill held the basket. The only damage was to her pride, although she had a red ring around her skinny buttocks. She scrambled to pull her panties up, then like an angry child, she leaped on the bed and turned a hateful face toward us.

"I broke my f---ing finger," she screamed, "and I'm going to sue you!"

Bill struggled to pull the basin, with its length of pipe attached, out through the door and into the hall. There he found a group of onlookers gathered at the top of the stairs attempting to peer into the room.

"Anyone get hurt?"

"Not yet," I said. "I am sorry that I have been so hospitable to that woman."

I was glad that the water had been turned off to that room. During all of this fuss, the man lay on the bed with his eyes open, still too drunk to get involved.

I closed the door on the disgusting woman.

I guess in her condition I should not have expected her to read the sign. I duteously emptied the waste basket.

When we returned to the saloon and told the story of our experience, the laughter grew in volume until someone alerted us that the skinny woman dressed in red was coming down the stairs… but now she was singing.

Into the saloon she sailed, like a ship with red sails, happy to be un-anchored, and friendly as a kindergartner. She was smiling, greeting everyone as if they were old acquaintances.

"On, no," Emmy whispered to me. "I am not going to put up with any more from her. I know what I'll do; I can send her across the street. My husband is the bartender tonight at Vim's club; let him deal with her. Emmy proceeded to speed to a woman seated at the bar, knowing that this woman would enjoy the joke. Together they planned to invite the woman in red, across the street for a real drink! The plan was to then abandon her there. The invitation worked.

I felt uneasy about this, but said nothing. It wasn't a nice thing to do, to take advantage of this poor drunk fool. But then, I wasn't the woman's keeper. I watched her as she wandered into Vim's club. It as a shabby thing to do, to treat a hotel guest this way. I did feel that she would be safe and with caring people, and one of us would watch out for her.

I knew that it would have to be Bill, because I would have to go to bed soon in order to get up at 5 a.m.

The next morning as the café filled with familiar faces, I noticed that there was an unusual amount of laughter, for this early in the morning. Also the mention of a woman staying at the hotel. That is when I asked, "What's going on? What's so funny? Are you talking about the woman who sat on the wash basin and broke it off the wall?"

"No, the best thing she did happened across the street," Don said. He could hardly continue because of his chuckling. As he laughed, the funny picture of what had happened became a scene in the minds of the others, and they also laughed heartily.

"Well, tell me!" I pleaded.

"The woman walked into Vim's," Don began. "Leaning against the bar was the chief of police. He was standing with arms folded, as he spoke to the bartender. The woman in red kept staring at him. Even though he was dressed in his uniform, the woman closer to him making crude sounds like, 'wow,' and 'hmm,' in regards to his maleness."

"How do you like truck drivers?" she asked him.

"I have no trouble with truck drivers," he said, glancing in her direction, then back to his interrupted conversation.

The woman persisted.

"How do you like lady truck drivers?"

Before he could answer, she reached for and grabbed him by his private parts.

Someone else interrupted Don's story, adding, "At that point, even the jukebox died!"

Don continued, "Everyone in the bar watched those two. They were locked in a very strange position; he was hunched over like Quasimodo, and she calmly weighed his package in her hand."

The chief looked at the woman and noticed that she wore no shoes.

"Are you staying at the hotel?" he asked her.

"You bet your sweet ass I am! Oh, excuse me," she corrected. "I mean, you got that right."

"If you don't let go of me, you're going to spend the night in jail. You have had too much to drink tonight. Now you go back to the hotel and to your room. You understand me?" The chief said in a quiet but threatening voice.

She took her hand away from his crotch and saluted him, saying, "Aye aye, captain!"

We thought that was a very funny incident and we tried not to giggle when the chief came into the café. We found that he was trying to hide a grin and really didn't mind discussing the matter. As it turned out, the woman did not heed the chief's warning, but he did not carry out his threat to incarcerate her. At 2 a.m. Bill and Morgan, another of our bartenders, retrieved her from Vim's Club.

The next morning, the woman's partner, having had a night's sleep, ate an early breakfast and went to check on his truck which was in the parking lot at the market. At 11 a.m. we got word from Eva that the woman in red was coming down the stairs.

"She waved her hands at me," Eva said. "She told me that she would give me all of her diamonds for my clean slacks."

The cook and other waitresses couldn't resist going to the lobby to take a look at her as she descended the stairs. Her red outfit was terribly stained and wrinkled.

"I'll give you all of my diamonds," she repeated.

The young women rushed back into the kitchen giggling from the hilarity of the situation. I looked at each of them. Eva was so short that her slacks would have been of peddle-pushed length on the woman. The cook was wide around the middle, and waitress very tall. My slacks were the only choice; after all, I did have another pair upstairs.

I called, "How many diamonds does she have? I'll give her mine!" Then just to tease my workers, I started to remove my slacks.

"No, Milly, keep your pants on," these words caused a commotion in the café. When a few of the patrons peered over the swinging doors into the kitchen, I changed my mind.

Instead, I felt sorry for the woman. I went to her, telling her about a dress shop next to the hotel, where she could buy a pair of slacks and a shirt. She never did get herself cleaned up. Later that afternoon I was told that the two had climbed into the truck and were headed for a place called Rancho Murrieta. It was only a short distance from the hotel, but a long way from being the same.

Rancho Murrieta is a fancy golf course and social club. It also has expensive homes with green velvet lawns, tennis courts and swimming pools. Bill and I thought that perhaps we should telephone there to advise them of the approaching bedlam, but we reconsidered. Why should they be spared such a charming experience?

"Nah, let them find out for themselves. That truck won't get past the front gate." I said.

"Unless they are members!" Bill joked.

Chapter 24: The Hotel and Children

One night as Bill was closing up the saloon, another room #4 renter complained that the little white-haired man kept bothering him by walking into the room and waking him up.

"That guy seems to know exactly when I am going back to sleep," the guest said.

Bill returned the man's money and he quickly locked the saloon. At last, perhaps he had an opportunity to experience this phenomenon of a ghost... spirit... thing. He rushed up stairs to the room.

The odor in the room was that of one heavy with dust, like a room that had been closed for a long time. He pulled the bedspread over the pillows and lay down. There was a glare from the light on the stairs landing shining through the transom.

As he lay there waiting and listening, hoping that the ghost would come in, a peaceful calm came over him. The door rattled. He pretended to be sleeping, breathing heavily to accentuate his impression of a man heavily asleep.

The bed shook as if a heavy truck had rumbled by, and then everything became quiet again. The silence was amazing because the hotel was never quiet, with refrigerator motors, toilets flushing, and people coming home; and yet that evening it was quiet. Bill studied the room looking for a figure but detected nothing. After a half hour he left; I guess even the spirit knows better than to pull the boss' feet.

We didn't have many children visiting in the hotel, so for us, it was a particular delight. We discovered an unusual phenomenon. It wasn't anything that we adults could see,but it became more evident each time we had a young visitor that the spirits liked children.

A young mother drove from Los Angles bringing her new baby, and also her mother-in-law. This was their third visit to her husband, who was imprisoned at The Preston School of Industry. Each visit, they had reserved room #3, as it was our only room containing the two double beds.

They would arrive early Saturday morning and leave late on Sunday afternoon. They were delightful people and we looked forward to their stay. I sometimes arranged my time so that I might join them for coffee. On one of those occasions they told me quite unexpectedly about a remarkable experience that happened in their room.

Each time the baby cried or became fussy, the bed on which the baby was lying was gently rocked. Since this had also happened during their last visit, they were interested to see if it would happen again. This time, the bed was rocked and they heard a song being softly hummed.

I met another couple admiring the staircase. The girl with them was about ten years old, blind, and her speech was inaudible soft mumbles.

The woman asked me to tell them the history of the hotel, and while I did the girl began to make noises, as if someone was disturbing her. She squirmed, ducking her head as if drying to dodge a hug. She smiled and a deep-voiced laugh came from her throat. The man and woman looked both pleased, and surprised.

"This place has good vibes. Sara likes it here!" the man said.

109

As we continued to talk, I watched the girl. A happy expression would come across her face, and she would also brush her cheek with her hand. She finally seemed too tired and became frustrated, making whining sounds.

The man and woman seemed oblivious to her discomfort, and asked for more hotel information. I put my arm around the girl, and maneuvered her closer into the group. The girl became quieted. I must admit that I was fascinated with her actions.

When they had gone, I said, "Thank you, that was kind of you," just in case I wasn't wrong in believing that some unseen spirit cared about children.

Chapter 25: Tommy and Room #12

Tommy Thompson lived at the hotel in room #12 for more than a year. After he moved away, he knew that he could still depend on Bill and I to offer him a place to sleep if he should take one drink too many while visiting the bars in Ione.

One Saturday night, when he left Vim's Club and walked to his truck, he saw that one of our police officers had parked the patrol car right behind it. Until that moment, Tommy was intending to drive the six miles to his new home.

Calling him by name, the officer asked, "Are you planning on driving home?"

Not wanting to be challenged as to his sobriety, Tommy answered, "Not tonight, I have a room at the hotel!"

"Good," said the officer. "That was smart thinking."

But Tommy did not have a room. He was hoping that Bill or I would be around to tell him that his old room had not been rented. He didn't count on the fact that the kind officer wanted to see that he made it safely up the stairs. The policeman followed him into the hotel

Of course, Tommy didn't want the officer to know that he had lied so up the stairs they climbed. Tommy said, "You don't have to come up with me."

The officer motioned Tommy to keep moving.

As he waked toward room #12, Tommy was starting to worry. Suppose there was a lady in there and she screamed when he opened the door? In that case, he was afraid that he would go to jail for lying. If there is a man in the room, he figured that he might get a punch in the mouth, and then still go to jail.

"Here it is! This is my room." Tommy pointed to the number.

The officer waited. Tommy turned the knob and pushed the door. It wasn't locked. Reaching into the room, he flipped on the light switch and found the bed empty.

"Good night, officer," Tommy said as he stepped inside and closed the door.

He knew that the officer was still standing in the hall, so to help convince him that this indeed was his room, Tommy turned off the light. I'll just wait him out, he thought. When he leaves I can go and ask Bill if I can use my old room tonight.

The officer walked toward our apartment and tapped on the door. When Bill opened it and saw the officer, he became alarmed that perhaps something was wrong.

"There is no problem," the officer said. "But Bill, do you have a man named Thompson staying here?"

"Thompson?" Bill contemplated the name for a minute, before saying, "No, he died about a year ago!"

"I've heard storied about the ghosts in the hotel," the officer said. "This one is alive, however. I just left him in room #12."

"Room #12," Bill thought again. He knew that we had not rented that room. Then the idea came into his mind.

"Oh, that Thompson! Do you mean Tommy Thompson? That's his room all right."

The officer was doing his job well by trying to keep sleepy drivers off the road. When he left, Bill opened the door to room #12 and said, "Hey, you're in for the night. I thought that little white lie was better than a little gray cell."

"You got that right! Thanks, Bill," Tommy whispered.

Chapter 26: The Mo-Fo Men

I couldn't believe it… by this time we had thirteen of those mysterious dishes. I hope that this means "good luck."

In 1980, Bill and I rented a small apartment in Jackson. Living where you work is not a good idea. Besides the hotel being noisy, at night we found ourselves listening for sounds of trouble. Something was always needed our attention.

When we left for our apartment, although we rarely left together, we knew that the hotel was in good hands. Every one of our employees was the best, and could handle any emergency without contacting us.

One night Bill left at 10 p.m. heading for the apartment for a little quiet time and freedom from the usual anxiety. At 1:15 a.m., I am finally finished in the kitchen. All was quiet in the hotel as I climbed the stairs on my way to bed – I was going to stay there for the evening. I begin to think of how nice a small glass of chilled wine would taste.

Instead of going into our saloon, I went across the street to Vim's club. I knew that my friend and former waitress Judy was the bartender on duty that night. I was glad to find her with only one customer, and she seemed to be grateful for a little sober conversation.

The disturbing clatter of motorcycles made us glance at each other with apprehensive expressions.

"Should I flick off the open sign?" Judy teased.

"Yes," I whispered. When I heard the sound of heavy boots behind me I added, "And maybe you should have locked the door."

A young woman, who might have weighed 90 lbs., had on enough leather clothes, hair, chains, earrings and boots, to add 40 pounds of bulk to her petite body. The blue bandana hugging her forehead helped to contain her long black hair.

The other lone bar patron said good night, and Judy and I were alone with the woman in black.

Judy walked to the middle of the bar and asked, "Do you want a drink?"

"No, I can't drink. I'm the banker!" she said, as if Judy should have known.

"Is there a motel around here?" she asked, her husky voice sounding weary.

"No," Judy answered she glanced at me. "Just a hotel."

I don't know why, but I raised my nostrils in disgust at the thought of this person as a guest.

Three more people arrived, also dressed in black leather. The sound of their heavy boots resounded on the bare wooden floor of the cavernous room. I seemed to be a distant observer of a cast of characters in a scenario. I noticed that the arrival of the trio caused the tiny woman, the banker, to become agitated. She whacked at the bar with a black draw string purse – leather, of course.

"There's no f---ing motel in this God-damn town," she yelled, as if she were trying to speak above the cycle engines' roar. "I told you assholes, but no, you don't listen to me, do you?" She emphasized her though of their brain function by bending forward and imitating a chimpanzee.

The men ignored her, and with bored expressions turned toward the bar. One of them wore a long hair braid. It was heavy and straight down his back, reaching below his belt. The other two were the same type of person without anything distinctive about them.

The man wore a black knit hat that covered his ears. Hanging on to his arm was a pretty blonde woman, which my husband would describe as a dumpling, all rosy cheeks and dimples and still carrying too much of her baby fat.

The men ordered beer for themselves, one for the blonde, and a soda for the banker.

"No beer for you," Judy said, as she put the drink in front of the banker, "but I'll take some money."

The woman opened the leather bag and extracted the money for the round.

"It's raining like hell out there. Where are we gonna sleep?" the braid asked.

Judy looked to me for an answer. Heaven knows, I didn't want them. Still I found myself inviting them to stay. "I have rooms at the hotel!"

"What the hell will we do with a hotel room?" the braid asked.

"Sleep," I answered.

"Bullshit, I'm not leaving my hog out in the rain!"

"We don't allow animals in the hotel," I said hoping for a laugh.

No one heard me, because were suddenly shouting at each other.

The dimpled dumpling told the banker, "Now honey, let's go and look at the place, maybe it will be okay."

"Are you nuts," said the knit hat. He looked at her as if she had suggested making love in the poison oak bush.

"Listen carefully," he continued, as he stared into her face. "Motel, one door, one window, parking space right outside. Hotel, room upstairs. We wouldn't hear anyone messin' with the bikes." He glared at her, waiting for an answer, but she just lowered her head, having been reminded of how dumb he though she was.

"I am going to find a motel. Who's coming with me?" No one moved. He bounded off out of the door.

"Let him go," the braid said. "He won't go far, he never does. Can we go see the hotel lady?"

As we stood in the hotel lobby, I do not know why I said, "You could walk the bikes in here! Then you would be sure that no one will bother them."

I watched the braid. He rolled his eyes up toward the balcony.

"Which room would we have?"

"Up there Room #13, and over there," I turned and pointed, "Room #4." He paced around the lobby, while the women stood like rag dolls waiting to be set on a shelf. If he decided that the hotel wouldn't do, I knew that I would feel relieved. If he thought that it was okay, then I could not back out of my offer. As the moments passed, I begin to think that perhaps I could tell him that I remembered it was against the law to have a gasoline engine in the lobby – at least with the Ione Fire Department."

He finally asked to see the rooms, so I led them upstairs and opened the doors for them to take a look.

"This will do," he said. "I'll go and get my bike."

"I'll need $25.00 for each room," I said.

"Ask her, she's the banker," he shouted as he skipped down the stairs. After the woman paid for the rooms, I directed them to the bathrooms. Since the bathrooms are one on each side of the hall and back to back, I could hear their conversations through the wall as they talked.

"Is that bathroom as ugly as this one?"

"I guess!"

116

I made sure that they both went into the correct rooms. They giggled at the rooms' old fashioned style, while I was certain that they had both slept in worse places.

I went down the stairs and out onto the sidewalk to direct the braid.

"Go to the end of the street," I told him. "There is no curb there and the bike can easily be rolled up onto the sidewalk." I opened both of the hotel's front doors and watched as a well-kept Harley Davidson was wheeled carefully through them. I had never realized how wide one of them is.

In the lobby, he parked it and asked for newspaper, which he folded and placed it under the bike.

"In case the oil should drip, it won't dirty the carpet," he said.

"Thanks for caring."

He smiled at me and leaped up the stairs taking giant strides. I didn't mention to the blonde that the room she had chosen, #13, might give her an uncomfortable feeling if she were superstitious. The banker in room #4, our officially haunted room, caused me no worry; I knew that the ghost only bothered men who slept alone in the bed.

Hearing the roar of a motorcycle engine, I ran down the stairs and out to the sidewalk. The wayward knit hat had returned. He turned off the noisy engine and looked up at me as I stood on the curb, eighteen inches above the street.

"Where is the other bike, did they leave?"

It felt wonderful being in control of this tough type. As I looked down on him, I wanted to tell him that the others had gone to find a hotel. Instead I found myself telling the truth again.

"The other bike is in the lobby. Your friends are getting ready for bed, but I don't want you in there you look like trouble."

"Trouble... me?"

117

"Yes, you! You're the kind of man who likes to argue and fight."

"No, you got me all wrong," he said in a whiny voice. "I'll be good."

I was sure that if I didn't let him in, he would wake up the town complaining about it.

"Okay, walk the bike to the end of the street, and up the sidewalk."

Once again, I opened the doors. This bike was also in show-off condition. As he moved it into the hallways light, I could see the emblem on the back of his jacket, in a circle it read: *Mo-Fo Men, West Virginia.*

He parked the bike alongside the other one, and placed a piece of newspaper underneath.

"You're a nice lady," he said.

"Thank you, now get to bed. It's up there," I pointed again. "Room #13 or #4 over there."

He took a plastic rose from the handle bars and handed it to me. "What's your, name?"

"Milly!"

I didn't want to start a conversation with this guy.

"They call me Web – that's short for Webster."

He reached into a saddle bag and took out a small flat can and he withdrew a hand rolled cigarette.

"You want a joint?" he asked, offering me marijuana.

I glanced at the gift, and I was stuck, for words. I didn't want to hurt his feelings, but I also didn't want to sound stuffy and unknowing. Since I have never used tobacco, I certainly didn't want that junk either.

"Oh, no thanks. I only smoke the ones in the pink paper." Why did I say that? I thought that if I lived through the evening, I'd have to have my head examined.

"I've never heard of that kind; if you change your mind let me know." He removed his hat and tossed the marijuana into it.

118

His tousled brown hair stood up in points. I looked into his face and I was amazed at how young he was. He might have been a little way out of his teens, but his demeanor made him seem very mature.

I have always felt that this type of man was what the pirates of old were like. Two hundred years ago everyone feared them. The only difference was their mode of transportation. Not so tough, I mused as I lead him up the stairs. When we reached the landing, I casually asked, "Which woman is yours?" I asked, in order for me to direct him to the proper room.

"The sexy blonde. She's my woman."

I sailed forth with confidence on my last mission of the evening – to place this guy in the arms of his sweetie. Then I could finally go to bed. As I stepped into the open doorway of room #13, I was shocked to see, the braid and the blonde on the bed in an embracing position as they played kissy-touchy-feely.

"What the hell are you doin' with my woman?" Web shouted.

"Something that you can't do," the man with the braid said. "I'm lovin' her."

"You son-of-a-bitch, stand up."

Before the braid could extract himself from the arms of the blonde, Web had leaped on top of both of them and he was punching away at any part of their bodies that he could reach.

The blonde started to scream. I thought about my other guests. This commotion would definitely wake them up.

I ran to use the phone in our apartment and dialed the police station's number. The sheriff's office answers the phone at that late hour, and then relays a message to the Ione Police.

When the phone was answered, I told the dispatcher who I was and where the hotel was located.

119

"I have two Hell's Angel types fighting in one of my rooms."

It is strange how the name of one organization so accurately describes another.

"I also have three truckers sleeping in the hotel and if they wake up, I may have a bigger problem on my hands. Send an officer quickly!"

The scuffling was still going on, but I knew the officer would be here soon. Now I was scared as well as tired. I was also angry at Web, because he had promised to be good.

I stood in the doorway feeling helpless. I wished I had not been so soft-hearted, and then thought that soft-headed was the right expression. In the past when I have been involved in a problem, although nothing like this, I have jokingly called on the comedian Phyllis Diller to help me. I once heard her say in an interview, "Just say your line; if the audience doesn't laugh, get off the stage."

I felt a breeze pass by me, as if the front door had opened, but I heard nothing.

I bellowed from the doorway, "I did you two a favor. Is this the way you return it? Stop this right now, or I'll come in there and smack the hell out of both of you!"

They sat up, and began to laugh at my silly threat. At that moment, their heads were banged together, as if they were being used as cymbals.

They looked at each other with confused expressions, while rubbing the tender place on their heads and wondering, how that could of happened.

"Thanks!" I said aloud.

"You're welcome," they answered.

I wasn't thanking them, but the spirit whom I was sure had come to my assistance and given them the whack that I had wanted to.

"You are right, mom." The braid said. "We'll stop." I felt someone standing close behind me, and heard, "What a couple of assholes."

I knew who it was. I was surprised to see that the tiny woman was much thinner than I had thought. Now she was dressed only in underwear and boots. She sauntered back across the hall and into her room. I turned back to the three people in the room. The men were sitting on the edge of the bed passing the marijuana cigarette back and forth. The blonde had turned her back to them and appeared to be asleep.

"Okay, it's time to choose your room," I said in my most threatening voice.

"I am in mine." Web said, and he quickly lay down. The braid tickled him saying, "You win!"

I told them where to find the bathroom, and that I didn't appreciate the people who would use the sink for a urinal.

I turned off the light, closed the door and showed the braid where to find room #4. Then I could finally go to bed.

As I lay down, I thought of Bill sleeping so peaceful in our Jackson apartment and how upset he was going to be that I didn't telephone him when I had a problem. And of course, for inviting the bikers into the hotel in the first place.

The next morning at the bottom of the stairs a small group of people stood silently, examining the cycles. As I walked into the kitchen the cook called to me, "Where are the "Hell's Angels?"

The waitress added, "We were afraid to walk through the lobby this morning!"

I smiled at them, hoping that my calm attitude would relieve their anxiety.

"They are still upstairs, I guess! But they are *Mo-Fo Men from West Virginia*," I offered.

"One motorcycle group is like another; they are all Hell's Angels to me," the cook said, as she continued to attend to a grill full of pancakes.

"A horse and a cow are both animals, but they are not alike," I told her. "I'm tired; I need my morning coffee! Excuse my goofy answer, please!"

"We need a Harley Davidson in the lobby every morning. Business has been great this morning," the waitress said.

"You know how fast news travels!"

"Faster than a Harley. Why are people so interested in a motorcycle in the lobby? I wonder what a hog would rent for," I said, picking up Web's language, just to act smart and to get a laugh. "If it isn't too expensive, I might give the idea a try."

As I went into the café several customers asked me why I let the Hell's Angels park their bikes in the lobby. I said, "I guess that I asked them in because this is a hotel. It was raining! If you owned an expensive machine, wouldn't you want to keep it dry, and safe from vandals?"

I was trying to wake up and not become involved in conversation with the customers. I sipped coffee while thinking where I might find a cozy hideaway. The door to the lobby opened and the braid was motioning to me. He had a towel around his neck and his long hair was hanging loose over his shoulders like a brown cape.

An entire group of customers leaned to one side to get a look at this character while they sounded an, "Oh-oh" in unison. They became very interested in the hotel's business for a moment in time.

"Do you need a few more towels?" I asked.

"No, come out here. Our banker has lost her purse, and all of our money was in it."

I wondered if he was serious as I looked into his face. Was he going to ask if they might have the rent money back now that they were destitute?

I went up the stairs and into room #4 where the tiny woman, her head bowed in dejection, was seated on the bed. Her face was streaked with tears, while new ones were continuing to fall. She answered my questions.

"No, I didn't leave it in the bathroom! And no, I didn't take it across the hall."

"Did you put it under the mattress?" I asked. "That is what I would have done with it. I would have slept on it."

"No, I wouldn't do that!" she said through the tears.

I sighed. "Let me try something. All right, George," I spoke into the air, trying to lighten the moment. "If you have it, give it up!"

I pushed my hand far into the mattress, and to my surprise, there it was.

"Who's George," she asked, as I dragged the purse out.

"George is my guiding spirit. I can call on him anytime to help me find things." I lied, like you would to a child about the tooth fairy. George was a spirit all right, but he hadn't guided me to anything until now.

"I wish I had a guiding spirit!" she smiled, relieved to have the bag with the money in it wrapped around her wrist.

"I will give you George!" I said; we shook hands.

"Thanks, lady," she leaned forward and kissed my cheek

The braid looked bewildered. "We looked under the bed; we didn't see it!"

"You have to be pure of heart, and have only kind thoughts!"

Why was I talking to these two adults as if they are eight-year-olds? I must be more tired that I realized. I know for sure that I was tired of solving their problems.

"How about a reward?" the braid remarked.

"No thanks, I did nothing that any other hotel owner wouldn't have don't. How much money is in there?" I asked. I knew that our insurance would not have covered its loss, since I was not put into the safe.

"There is $400.00 in there," said the braid, "and that is enough to buy your breakfast, I won't hear you say 'no,' will I?"

"Okay, that is my favorite restaurant," I said as I pointed down the stair.

We were joined by the blonde and the knit hat.

"Did you make your bed?" I asked her.

She gave me the stunned look of a cat who had just been scared at its reflection in a mirror.

She drew a breath. "No," she said as she covered her moth with her hand and looked at her companions for a signal that they had or had not made theirs.

Now I was getting silly. I desperately needed some coffee. It would calm me down and protect these people from my devilish wit. I led the four into the café. The hum of voices became hushed until we sat down; then the breakfast-eaters took up were they left off, discussing us in general, and me in particular.

One of Ione's older women called me to her table. "Who are your friends?" she asked.

Her voice had an assumption of superiority that affected my opinion of her.

"Just hotel guests who have enjoyed their stay so much, that they have promised to tell all of their friends to come to Ione. The man with the long hair says that this looks like an easy town where a man could rape and pillage."

She knew that I was being sassy, and she smiled a soft tolerating smile, and then cautioned me to be careful.

Of what? I thought of this as I sat down. If one of these people should stab me with a butter knife, she has my permission to telephone the police, but they probably wouldn't come anyway.

Thank goodness my coffee arrived at the table. The rest of the cafés patrons would safe from my sardonic humor.

When it came time for the Mo-Fo Men to leave, I asked that they not start up the cycle engines in the lobby.

Propping open the hotel's double door again, I could look outside to see that my guests had attracted quite a few onlookers. Ione citizens stood along the curbs as if they were waiting for a parade. The window in the coffee shop across the street was more crowded than usual.

"You have a large audience out there," I said to Web.

"Oh yeah, I'll just have to give them a show! I can jump the curb for them."

"No," I pleaded. "My god, don't do that. The curb is very high, as you already know; you could fall off the bike and break your back. Then the bike would be out of control and might crash though that window," I said pointing across the street. It could land in the laps of those coffee drinkers."

Web started the engine.

"I asked you not to do that!" I shouted above the roar. He was lost in a world of noise, grandiose stunts, and cheering crowds. In his imagination he could probably see his name twinkling in Las Vegas lights, but he sure didn't hear my little voice.

The hotel reverberated from such a loud sound in such a confined space. Every door rattled. Men stood above us looking over the railing, sleepy-eyed, dressed only in their underpants.

Web was off, racing down the hallway toward certain death. I ran after him. He burst out onto the sidewalk, the bike stopping suddenly at the curbs edge. I saw everyone who was sitting within the window frame of the restaurant across the street stand up as if doing the wave at a ball game.

I rushed out to stand at his side. My heart was in total alarm.

"Fooled you," Web said and grinned at me. He backed the bike away from the curbs edge, and then with the engine still running, he stepped off of the bike and proceeded to wheel it down the sidewalk. By the time the braid emerged, with his long hair blowing wildly, there was a larger crowd on each side of the street.

The bikes attracted attention while parked in front of the hotel, where the men sat along the curb talking to those who asked questions of them. The blonde re-braided the beautiful hair that was put before her, as the man sat on the curb between her legs. No questions were asked, no excuses were given. She did it automatically, lovingly, brushing it and winding it into a thick braid, securing it with a rubber band. People stood silently and watched as if they had never seen this done before.

Ione's walking newspaper, the town gossip, ran to the police station to tell them that the Hell's Angels were riding on the sidewalk, and almost ran over her. This is the same woman who called to inform me that, room #4 could not be haunted by George's ghost because he didn't die in that room, but in the hospital. She knew, because she had gone to the hospital with him and his room was #5. Hmmm.

A year later, as I crossed the street I saw two motorcycles, parked in front of the hotel and I heard, "Hey look, there's mom!"

"Hey mom, haven't they run you out of town yet."

The Mo-Fo Men were back. The braid stepped down from the curb and picked me up, carrying me into the saloon. It was the first time that I had introduced someone to my husband while I was being held in their arms. Bill felt better about the incident after meeting them. Well, a little better.

One mystery was what had happened to the policeman that I had called for that first evening. I did complain to the chief of police, who was quite upset at hearing of my dilemma, but he had no answers. He made an inquiry into the matter, and informed me later in the day that the officer had come by the hotel and all was quiet.

Perhaps if the officer had walked in when the men were having their tussle, his appearance could have made the situation worse. Had I mentioned on the phone that I had been offered marijuana, I would have probably had police, sheriff and maybe the narcotics squad causing a black-booted ruckus on the stairs.

Looking back, I'm glad that the officer didn't come in.

Chapter 27: The Little Boy Ghost

A couple who had spent a weekend with us two years earlier returned to introduce their two-year-old daughter. She toddled around the lobby with an adult always in pursuit to keep her from scampering up the staircase. Her daddy would carry her back under the stairs to where her mother, grandmother and I were chatting. The child insisted to be on the run, however, and was once again set upon her fast little feet.

This time she grabbed the drape which hung along the back wall of the lobby. Pulling it aside she looked behind it and said, "Peek."

Giggling with delight, she dropped the curtain and scampered away. We were bewildered when the curtain followed her, attempting to whack her on the bottom before it fell limply back into place. At that moment we all joined the gasp and shrug club while her father, thinking someone was hiding beneath the curtain, lifted it to investigate this weirdness. The area showed no reason for the action!

The child was so amused with the game that she repeated the same act. Once more the curtain chased the child. After the toddler recovered from her laughing and excitement, she lifted the curtain and walked behind it.

We watched her feet as they moved along below the curtain. Could she be seeing someone who, as adults, we could not see? Her body wiggled and she made sounds as if she were being tickled. She became quiet, and hurriedly reappeared. Going directly to her mother, she pleaded to be picked up. Her mother hugged her lovingly and reassured the child, saying, "You are having a good time. Mommy's got you now!" and kissed her on the cheek.

The child looked into her mother's face and waving one hand toward the curtain, said, "Bad boy!"

I thought that was a strange expression for her to say toward an empty space, behind a curtain. Perhaps she was playing with the little boy ghost, only he didn't have enough energy to appear in body form or we would have seen him.

I have known of children who talked to invisible playmates. Perhaps children have the ability to see spirits, an ability they eventually outgrow.

The young man who worked for us each night cleaning the kitchen was a pleasant person. He and I had great conversations while we worked and listened to his favorite rock music.

One day we had received a large delivery of meat and groceries, so he had stacked all of the empty boxes in the back hall against the kitchen door.

As he mopped around the appliances, stooping to do a good job, he straightened up and said, "Who's that?"

"Where?"

"That little kid! He's looking at me, right there in the take-out window!"

I glanced around the dish shelves to get a look at who he saw; I saw no one.

"Wow, he's gone! Honest, he was smiling at me. He had on a blue shirt."

"It must have been our little boy ghost," I suggested.

"I saw him, he was real!"

"Why don't you go and try to find him?"

My husband Bill chose to visit us at that particularly uneasy moment. He unlocked and pushed open the kitchen door, causing the stacked boxes to tumble. With one great leap my unbelieving cleanup worker leaped with a giant exuberant thrust over the top of a very full garbage can like a high jumper.

"I'm finished, see you later," he called as he ran out the front door. He was really finished. The next day, he phoned to say, "My grandmother says that I can't work at the hotel any longer. She doesn't want me to work at a place that has spirits; she believes all spirits are bad and come from the devil. Also, she says that you should try to get rid of them." She offered no instructions on how to do this.

Chapter 28: A Day for Religion

I moved carefully between the dining room tables as I placed the rust-colored napkins on the gold tablecloths.

"This looks great!" said a husky male voice.

I turned to face a pleasant looking man, wearing a cap and soft wool clothes as if he were about to go for a leisurely walk. I watched him and waited for more conversation, while he lit the pipe which he had placed to one side of his mouth.

I didn't wait any longer. "Are you passing through Ione?" I asked.

He puffed hard on the pipe, until he had to wave away the cloud of smoke that permeated the air with a rich, sweet tobacco odor. Then he said, "I'm on my way back to Sacramento; I just stopped into the café," he motioned with his thumb, as if explaining to me where it was. "They make a pretty good steak sandwich."

"It had better be good, or I will have to talk to the cook. I'm Milly, and I own the hotel." We shook hands.

"Walt Wiley," he said. "I didn't know this room was back here!"

"This dining room has been here for almost two years."

"I noticed that the name of the hotel had changed," he said.

"We like *The Hotel Ione*. It's a little play on words."

"How is the hotel business?" he asked in a friendly manner.

"We have 100% occupancy," I bragged.

"Wow, I'm amazed. You sure can't do better than that," the man said.

"No, even if I wanted to, there are only eighteen rooms that we can rent. The rest are a linen room, an office, and three rooms for my husband and me to use. What this town needs is a motel. There are only men who rent rooms. I see them at breakfast, dinner and bar time. It works well, since they have only two bathrooms. They don't appreciate the tricks that our ghosts play on them, though."

He removed his pipe and grinned at me. His eyebrows raised. Closing one eye, he tilted his head and stared at me, like a one-eyed cyclops.

My response to his expression of disbelief was to tell him my collection of ghostly happenings.

"Milly, could I write about this?" he asked, reaching into one of his jacket pockets and brining out a pen and a tablet. "I write a column for the *Sacramento Bee*."

"If you did, that would be our first article in a newspaper outside of Amador County. I'll have to ask my husband, though. I'll be right back."

Bill said it would be all right with him, and I told him, "We can't knock the free advertising."

Since we agreed, the reporter wrote the story. The following Saturday morning, the lobby was crowded with people who had read Walt Wiley's column and were hoping to see a ghost for themselves.

"Where are the ghosts?" someone demanded.

"Unfortunately, I cannot call on the spirits to appear," I said with a shrug.

"What can you do? I drove forty miles from Sacramento to see them!" said a loud demanding voice.

"I can only explain my theory on the ghosts and spirits. There are many things that have to happen before we can witness or feel one," I said. "First of all we must consider the weather. Most ghost stories begin with a weather report." I thought a minute and recited the typical beginning of a ghost story.

"It was raining. Thunder crashed and lightning danced across the hilltop. The darkness hides the old mansion's dead and untidy garden. A dim light could be seen moving from room to room, although no one lived there." I had everyone's attention.

"This is not just to put you into a scary mood, it is a fact that depressed weather can cause spirits to move. We have all seen the painting of Christ. All show him with a glow around him. This is to represent his external energy, called an aura. We also have an aura, every living thing has one, even trees."

"I have a theory; when a person dies, this external energy, the aura, falls from the body. It stays in the room until it can gather enough energy from other sources, people. When the nightly TV weather report tells us that the barometric pressure is falling, like in the story, it could mean we will have rain. It will mean that the pressure falling will meet with the pressure which rises naturally from the earth, and the pressures will squeeze between them the energy that the dead person no longer needs. This causes these leftover auras which we call energy masses or spirits to move about. Gloomy days are the days when we have the most spirit activity. Once it is on the move, these energy masses can be found anywhere, and not necessarily just in old buildings. The reason most are found in old buildings is because in the olden days most people died at home. By the time the body was removed, the energy had time to free itself of the body that no longer had a need of it."

"This hotel has walls over a foot thick. The meager energy which these spirits have is not strong enough to let them pass through."

133

"Why don't they just go out the open door or window?" a woman asked.

"They would if they happened to be right there when the window or door is open," I replied. "If one floats past you, it will touch your own aura, and cause the hair on the back of your neck and on your arms to rise. The air around you may feel cold. That is because you are a little frightened about something that can touch you, but that you can't see."

"Because it is cloudlike," I continued, "it can become larger or smaller by blending into other spirits. They pick up the dust particles and smoke that causes their color to change from invisible, to white to light grey and charcoal, like the first one I met in the dining room."

"Since today is a sunny day, we won't be able to see one, but I can take you to where you might feel one." I held out my bare arm. "Push your sleeves up so; your arms will be bare, and follow me." I headed a train of sixteen whispering people who jostled each other to form a line.

As we turned the corner at the top of the stairs, I held my arms out at my sides and glanced behind me. We looked like a kindergarten class, imitating airplanes.

One of our regular guests walked out of his room dressed in robe and slippers, his towel and shower necessities in hand.

"Are you trying to find the ghost this morning?" he asked the group, "I hope he isn't in the shower. If I find him in there I'll tell him that you are looking for him."

As we moved slowly along the hall I asked them to tell me if they felt anything unusual. "A feeling of a sudden chill or the feeling of having put their hand through a spider's web. Your fingers may feel tingly."

Being the leader, and also knowing what sensation to react to, I found the energy mass first. I stepped aside not mentioning that I had found it. Some people can feel this and other cannot. I watched for the surprised open-mouthed expressions of amazement from such a peculiar feeling.

"Eeow," a woman said, as she shivered and closed her eyes, perhaps faring that something horrible would pop up in front of her. "It's there," she pointed to the wall.

"She is right," I told the group.

Everyone gathered close, trying to feel what she had.

"Stick your arm into it, right here." She grabbed another woman's arm, and waved it about.

"Oh," her friend groaned. "Yes, I can feel it. That is a strange sensation."

"It feels like a mild electric shock," a man said.

Another woman said. "Maybe it's a woman, and she doesn't like you getting personal." And playfully pulled the man's arm away from, the area.

"It is cold; why do I get goose-bumps from it?"

I shrugged. "That is one of the questions I have no answers for. Why do we all of a sudden get a shivering chill? You know, the one that catches you unaware while you are sitting quietly. My theory is that a spirit has passed by and touched your aura and made you jump. Since science can't explain this reaction, then that is a good theory until another idea comes along. Science can't find out where a cats purr comes from either."

"Here is some new energy," a man said, "It feels like static electricity. My shirt is going toward it."

"It also has your hair," I said.

He stepped back and ran his hand through his hair; other pushed forward to test the experience.

"Anyone afraid?" I asked.

"No," was the collective whisper.

As we walked down the stairs, one of the children trying to whisper to another child said, "Can the spirits come back to life, bite your neck and suck your blood?"

"No," I answered, then explained, "That only happens in the movies. That is why you go to the movies – to be scared. It is fun because you know the evil person can't come down off the screen and get you. It was only a picture of people in costume, just like you on Halloween. If someone made a movie about this hotel it would be interesting, but not scary... really kind of sweet.

"The spirits have made us laugh and they haven't hurt anyone. I think people who are afraid choose to be. I cannot explain why they are here teasing us in such a playful manner. My grandmother told me, 'God didn't want us to know everything, because our lives would be very dull with nothing to spark our curiosity.' I am happy to accept the things I cannot change. I guess spirits in an old hotel is one of those things."

As the group walked down the hall toward the exit, a larger group walked in. I made a dash into our kitchen for a glass of water.

The café was full, for its usual Saturday morning trade. I noticed two women sitting at one table. My intuition told me that they were tourists. We smiled and greeted each other. They stood up and walked toward the register, while I went back out to the lobby to the group of people around the stairway, where I answered questions. The ladies I had seen in the café were approaching me they were short, chubby and 35 to 40 years old. They wore printed silk jersey dresses, with cool linen jackets, nylons and flat shoes. I felt rather stupid and rude, as I excused myself pretending to have business elsewhere. Something about these two caused me to retreat into the dining room to arrange the tables that were already setting neat.

Soon the ladies were standing in the dining room, too.

"Hello," I said to them. Their quiet manner made me uncomfortable. They stood watching me, waiting... but for what?

I looked around at the tables, nodded once, smiled, and said, "Okay, this looks good." I then turned to the ladies. "What can I do for you?"

"Hello," they said in unison.

My unexplained nervousness had made me respond with a silly question.

"That was good, which one of you is the ventriloquist?"

They even giggled in unison.

"Are you Milly?"

"Yes, I am," I answered.

I wondered why these two wanted a private meeting.

"I am Sister Jaclyn and this is Sister Frances. We are from Wicca, in Sacramento!"

I had heard of this, it is the witches' coven of perhaps several hundred followers. I do know that it is just another religion, so I don't know why they made me uncomfortable.

"I have heard of your group. Why did you come here today?" I asked, as I shook hands with them.

We walked back out to the lobby where several people were ascending the stairs, with their arms extended.

"They're looking for spirits," I told the ladies. "Do you want to join them?"

"No," one of them said emphatically. "We read in the paper about the ghosts. You only mention seeing a few of them; we came to tell you that where there is one, there are many. Those stairs are crowded with them and we couldn't go up there because the ghosts wouldn't let us."

"Do you think they are evil?" I asked.

"Only time will tell. We certainly hope they aren't," one said.

The other woman added, "It has been nice meeting you, and we had a lovely breakfast."

"Thank you," I answered. "And thanks for the information." We shook hands again and they walked away. I would have liked to hear the conversation back at the witches' coven. I wonder what happens to the spirits on the stairs when we run the vacuum cleaner. Maybe that is the answer to why my vacuum cleaner acts like it wants to let things out instead of picking it up.

The same evening, Father Wall arrived with two visiting, very Irish, nuns. It has been a day for religion, I thought. This trio was anxious to know our spirits, so I took them into room #4, while I told them my most-repeated stories.

"These spirits cannot possible compare with the many you have in your Irish castles. You have the best ghost stories over there." I was attempting to flatter them, when one of the nuns asked, "Father, do you really believe in spirits?"

The father looked horrified for a moment, and then he patiently said, "You should also! Or return to the convent. We pray to a spirit."

The nun hid her face while she laughed in surprise and embarrassment. The poor woman was mortified. While we didn't want to ridicule her, we did find it difficult not to enjoy her innocent and mistaken words. Even the good father found it amusing and I'll bet he repeated the story.

Chapter 29: That's Incredible

The story of our hotel and its ghosts somehow came to the attention of Aaron Kass, executive producer of the television show *That's Incredible*. He phoned to ask if we would allow our hotel to be featured on the program. At that time in 1980 this was a very popular show.

Bill and I discussed it for two days, as we wondered if the publicity would be good for us or work against us. We talked with those employees who would be involved with the film, or at least would be interviewed. Judy, Eva, Chris. Our friend Jack, who no longer lived in the hotel. Bob, who had known the man named George and had identified him as one of our friendly spirits. Rachel, who had done such a good job as a medium. I also contacted the Johnsons. It had been two years since the ghost stood at the foot of their bed. All graciously agreed to be in the TV film.

The only person who complained was... guess who? The town gossip. She telephoned to say that it was terrible of us to bring such stupid notoriety to Ione. I told her she was absolutely right and thanked her for her opinion, and then we went on with our plans.

The TV crew began filming very early on June 21 and continued until midnight. Coincidentally, the next day was the third anniversary of the day that Stacy and I saw the first spirit

140

in the dining room; we wondered if it would appear again for the camera.

The television crew was headed by producer/director Ted Bateman. If his name sounds familiar to you, he has two famous children. Actress Justine, (*Family Ties*) and Jason Bateman, (*The Hogan Family*).

The first day we had to lock the hotel entry door and add a sign which read: *TV Show Filming, Quiet Please.* Bob Ketchem filmed his portion of the show while being interviewed in room #4 as he sat on George's bed. Perhaps the crew was waiting for the spirit to shake the bed. Bob told of his meeting and befriending George, and how he admired the man... And then how he had found him dead from a heart attack thirteen years earlier.

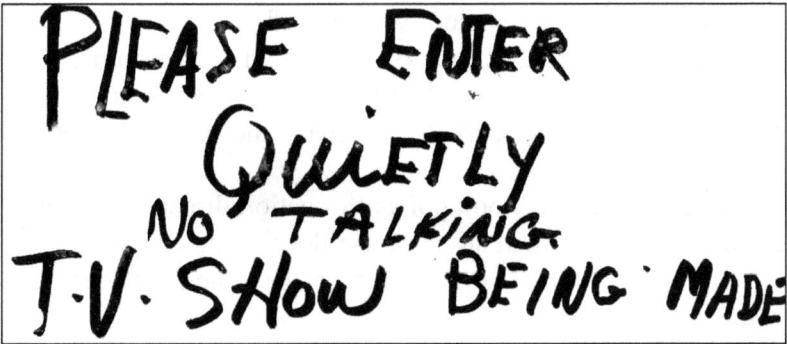

The Sign from the Front Door

Rachel, our medium, was pregnant and feeling ill. She was unable to tape her portion of the film until evening. I do not know what the director wanted her to say. It took such a long time to film her segment. She was positively ready to drop from exhaustion at midnight.

During the whole filming operation, everything that could go wrong, did go wrong. First we noticed that the monitor, a

141

small television screen which the director watches during the filming, was doing its own acting.

When I noticed the frustration in the directors' attitude, I guessed that a spirit was causing a problem. I suggested this to Mr. Bateman and he agreed to a trial use of draping a bedspread over the machine when it was not in use. This did not solve the problem of the unseen prankster who loved lights, dials and switches.

Before the Johnsons arrived, the film crew went into room #2. The idea was to get pictures of this room without guests and also to check the lightning. Would the room be too dark to get a clear picture?

At the moment the room looked great. The sun, beginning its descent, illuminated a small portion of the bed. The window was open about four inches and a draft of air fluttered the pink silk drapes each time the door was opened.

"This looks great," Ted Bateman said to the cameraman who stood nearby awaiting instructions. "Get a picture of that nice little fluttering curtain. It gives the room a homey, peaceful look!"

The cameraman stood poison for action directly in front of the door. Mr. Bateman stood at the door's hinged side, out of camera range, and with one hand he pushed the unlatched door open.

"Ready – the door is opening, the camera is rolling, the curtain should be fluttering." After a moment, he yelled, "Cut!"

The drapes hung listlessly. Ted Bateman laughed. He ran a hand through his hair, shrugged in disbelief and said.

"I've never seen an obstinate drape until now. Let's try again. The camera is rolling, the door is opening and the curtain is blowing. Beautiful, nice flutter, although, I wish it could flutter with a little more gusto!"

Suddenly the scene was quite different. The drapes were stretched ridiculously straight out from the rod, as if they were being held up by a playful spirit.

"Cut," Ted Bateman called. The drapes fell immediately into place.

"I've never seen drapes act on cue! Let's be finished with the window pictures; we can use whatever we were able to photograph, with or without the fluttering drape."

The Johnsons' segment, taken in the room with the drapes that could act on cue, only had to be filmed once. Mrs. Johnson was the one who scolded the ghost in her room, two years earlier while Mr. Johnson slept.

Filming *That's Incredible* at the Hotel Ione

The story of the boy ghost which I saw looking into the well interested Mr. Bateman and we recreated the scene. First we had to select a boy. We advertised by word of mouth. We chose Jerry; I was able to make him a costume of a blue shirt with a big collar and wide sleeves. With his hair combed into a bob-style, his resemblance to the ghost was startling.

It was my turn again. Standing in front of the refrigerator I told the story of how the forty-eight steaks had appeared mysteriously, giving us the seventy-two we had wished for.

We then went to the lobby, where they took pictures of eight-year-old Jerry, as he stood quietly looking into the well. He was being a stand-in for the boy ghost that I had seen. He was also the stand-in for the boy ghost that Jack saw looking at him through the screen door. He was photographed while Jack told of his experience. It was recreated with creepy reality.

On Monday, it was Eva's turn to act out her story. She arrived dressed in waitress attire of black slacks, white shirt and small taffeta apron. Ted Bateman put the large box of paper napkins outside of the linen room door; out of camera view, where they would be easy to get for re-stacking Eva's arms should the need arise.

As Eva stood at the top of the stairs, she told me that she was very nervous. I told her that I understood and that I had also been nervous. I explained that it was just acting out what happened when the napkins were knocked out of her hands, and that it wouldn't take very long.

The sun shone brightly, illuminating the whole lobby. The cameraman lay on his stomach at the foot of the stairs, with the camera propped up on a couple of books to correct the angle.

The monitor was working perfectly. No mischievous spirits were around to disturb the switches.

"Everyone quiet! The camera is rolling." The director waved to Eva. He had instructed her to look frightened and let the napkins fall when she reached the fourth step. He was trying to recreate the scary happening which she had experienced.

She was carrying five bundles of napkins, each of them wrapped only with a single band of paper. When she performed as instructed and dropped the napkins, they rolled like footballs still intact when they stopped.

They did that again on the next try. The director cut one of the bundles wrappers through, and perforated the others but the bundles never separated on their tumble. A ladder and a large window fan were ordered. These were placed alone the side of the staircase with the fan turned on blowing full speed. Now Mr. Bateman directed, "Okay, Eva, come down slowly; at the fourth step, you know what to do!"

She nodded that she understood, and down the stairs she stepped. We could not believe it since this was the eleventh time, but again nothing happened to disturb the packages of napkins.

"I don't know what else to do!" the director said. "This will be our twelfth and last attempt," he added. "If it does not happen this time we will just use your interview. Okay, ready, roll."

Eva came slowly down the steps. When she reached the third one, the napkins were punched out of her arms. She screamed and continued to do so. When the napkins exploded into the air and Eva's high pitched and frantic screams filled the lobby, director Batman ran from the lobby going down the hall toward the front door. I ran also, until we realized how silly we looked. We laughed and returned to the scene, where Eva sat on the stairs crying, and 1,500 napkins were still descending like doves. The entire lobby was littered and the strong breeze from the fan had flattened hundreds of napkins against the banister.

"Cut! Turn the fan off!"

We had forgotten about the cameraman who was still lying on his stomach. Now he rested his forehead on the camera. He

145

was still too startled from the occurrence he had just photographed.

"Milly," the cameraman said, "don't be mad at me if when I get up, there is a little brown spot here on the carpet. That was scary!"

"Believe me, I'll forgive you," I assured him.

I put my arm around Eva. "It happened again," she said through her tears.

"Yes but what a film," the cameraman added, "I'll be proud to have that one. I sure wish I had infra-red film and the proper light. I could have had a picture of the rascal who made this mess."

The entire next day was spent re-interviewing everyone, and photographing both inside and the outside of the hotel. Burned-out camera lights and spot lights were replaced at no charge by the local TV repairman. The Ione citizens were generous with their time answering questions. They crowded the saloon for a re-enactment of an Ione homecoming celebration.

Director Bateman told me a story of his waking up in his hotel room early one morning and seeing a large shadow on the wall. His first thought was that it was overcast, and he was disappointed. He was intending to do more outside filming. When he looked at the windows he was surprised to see bright sunshine and blue sky.

Being puzzled about this, he looked again at the wall and the shadow was gone. That is when he decided to get out of bed, no matter what time it was.

Saturday evening after 9 pm we did our last filming. The story of our still-growing glass dishes fascinated everyone. Director Bateman thought it would be nice to have the dishes on display in the antique candy case in the café. It had one long wooden shelf, which was the right high to photograph me through the front glass while I was looking through the glass case from behind. I was to look bewildered while counting the growing stack of dishes. I would have no trouble looking confused at this phenomenon.

I placed a few dishes into the case, and then the camera was turned off while a few more were added the stack. The camera turned on; once again I counted and found more dishes. The director was trying to show how the dishes have mysteriously arrived through the last three years. Beginning in 1977 with six, and by 1980 there were thirteen. When the slow process was done and all of the dishes were in the case, we waited with the camera running, hoping to catch something for the television audience. If not a picture of the generous spirit, then perhaps a dish arriving out of the air or however this happened. No more dishes appeared; *That's Incredible* packed it all up.

I sat on the lobby stairs and watched while the reels of film were put into a heavy wooden and metal box. Each in their own can, fitting neatly into a slot, all numbered and accounted for. The name of the person involved in that segment was printed on it also. The box was closed and padlocked, and was soon on its way to the Sacramento Airport for a flight to the studio in southern California.

The end of fifty hours of hard work was behind us. The making of a television show about the hotel Ione would play only seven minutes.

The next day was Sunday. After our usual whirlwind of a breakfast, Ione seemed to doze in the august heat. It was, if you'll pardon the pun, "Oh, so dead." Judy added, "If I didn't need the money I'd go home."

We had both been back and forth taking portions of the Sunday paper back to the table where we sat chatting and sipping coffee. Cal came in through the hall door. He relieved our monotony while he had a quick cup of coffee. Not finding our conversation stimulating, he left, crossing the hall to the saloon perhaps to find the guys to talk to.

Judy and I both groaned, expressing our boredom, and descending once again toward the front window to see if anything had changed outside.

We played 'identify that car' by guessing who the owners of the cars along the street were. The only places their owners could be was in one of the bars. I straightened the large Sunday paper, almost willing to read the sport section. When I moved the pile there was a glass plate under it.

"Darn it, who took this out? It is lucky that it didn't fall off and get broken" I said, as Judy looked at me and shrugged, expressing that she did not know.

"Can you believe this," I continued to berate the unknown person who did not read the sign on the back of the candy case which read: *Do not touch these plates!* As I placed the dish into the case with the others, a quick count told us that number fourteen had arrived.

Early on Monday morning, I received a phone call from Landsberg Productions.

"Mrs. Jones, have you found on of our reels of film? When the box was opened, one reel was missing. It is the one which has Bob Ketchem being interviewed."

The film was never found. Perhaps George, our resident ghost, was embarrassed about the kind and flattering stories told of his years in the hotel, ones his friends remember fondly.

On Tuesday morning, the wooden shelf holding the glass dishes somehow shifted and one end dropped, causing them to slide down its length. Two of them shattered. Even though I was very disappointed, it wasn't a tragedy to cry over. I had only asked for a dozen.

On October 2, 1980, *That's Incredible* aired the show with our seven minute segment about a Northern California haunted hotel. We watched it in the saloon, along with many of the people who were featured on the film.

We only caught a thirty-second look at Eva! She was seated at a dining room table, looking serious, while she answered one question.

"Have you had any weird experiences while working at the Hotel Ione?"

"Yes, I've had weird experiences while working at the hotel."

This brought a big laugh, and remarks about weird experiences having nothing to do with ghosts. The film went on to show an all-over view of our saloon, crowded with townsfolk. It also had scenes of the staircase and dark hallways and the Johnsons, telling their story about the old man who was in their room. We also showed them one of a picture of Jerry, looking into the well, and also one of Jerry looking through the screen door, as Jack told the story of the boy he saw and how the child's face melted away. There was a picture of the outside of the hotel and one of Bill saying in his most somber voice, "NO, I have never seen any ghosts."

There were pictures of me explaining a few strange occurrences and showing the glass dishes.

They did not show the real happening which they had on film – the part that had Eva coming down the stairs and having the napkins knocked out of her hands. There was no part of the interview taken with Rachel, the medium who helped us with the séance. Of course there was none of Bob's interview in George's room.

It seemed to me that the television show told nothing of what we have experienced with the spirits, or the hotel's personality or the fun we were having as we worked together.

While we were watching the show in California, the show had already been seen in other states. The phone began to ring, as people across the United States asked for reservations.

Tammy, our bartender, covered the phone's mouthpiece with her hand and asked, "How much for a room?"

"You know," I answered. "It's fifteen dollars a night!"

"Not anymore, it isn't."

Tammy spoke into the phone. "It's $25.00 a night. Give me your phone number, and we will call you back!"

"We don't have room for tourists," I complained.

Bill advised that we set up the reservations at our convenience. Assign a vacant room to each phone number. Call them, and find out when they want to visit. Ask that they mail us a, $10.00 non-refundable deposit.

All the phone calls were returned and we reserved five rooms for almost a year in advance.

What did those people see in that film that excited them? We received many letters from children; whole class rooms, in fact. I guess it was just that this seemed to be a place where guests and employees got along with a mysterious being, that could be experienced, and it wouldn't hurt you. Like Disneyland's Haunted House. Well, that is the right idea.

Chapter 30: A Hypnotic Invitation

A few days after the television show aired, Bill and I went to Sacramento to replace my broken eye glasses. Because there are so many optometrists there, we thought it unnecessary to make an appointment. Bill had received his glasses at a certain office and he had been treated very well, so we headed for that one. When we arrived we could see into the waiting room. It was packed with waiting patients.

"There must be another optometrist close by!" I said. As I looked at the list of Doctor's names, one attracted my attention.

"That one – Dr. Smith!"

"Okay, but why not find a Jones?" Bill kidded.

"I'm wondering if he is my friend from grammar school, Bunny Smith. I loved him because he could tap dance."

Bill laughed at me. "Are you going to ask the doctor if he can tap dance?"

"I might if he's as cute as a bunny, like he was when he was eight years old."

I filled out the questionnaire for the receptionist. Then I was taken to a room full of eye examination apparatus.

Dr. Smith came into the room, with his head down, intent on reading my information sheet.

"Hello Mildred," he said, still not looking at me. I was amazed; this guy could read, walk and talk at the same time without walking into walls.

"I'm Dr. Smith," he looked at me. "I see that you need new glasses."

"It seems so!" I handed him my broken glasses, which had one lens and one ear piece. Again he was studying the information sheet.

"Ione, Ione…" he repeated. "I recently heard something about the town of Ione."

It crossed my mind that perhaps he was thinking of the TV show.

"I know!" he said as he flashed a smile of relief at remembering, what he was trying so hard to recall. "It was on television, a haunted hotel. Do you know the people who own it? Are they kooky?" he asked, as he touched his temple with a finger.

"No, not strange at all; in fact, they are very nice."

"Then you know the TV program *That's Incredible!* had a segment about them on their last show! I didn't see it. I arrived late for a class I am taking at a San Francisco University. The class was all a buzz about the woman who owns the hotel. They believe that she has the power to conjure!"

"I do?"

He looked at me with shock and embarrassment.

"Wow me, I can conjure? Oh sure, me and Jesus!" I laughed out loud. Too loud for that small room.

"The class talked about contacting you and asking if you would consent to coming to San Francisco to be hypnotized."

"For what?"

"I guess to find out how your mind works; to make a study."

"They wouldn't want to waste the taxpayers money on my mind," I said.

On our way back home, I told Bill of the conversation with the Doctor. We both agreed that I should not be hypnotized.

The most religious person that I knew was the local priest. I always spoke to him when he ate dinner in the café. In the Bible, it tells how Jesus could conjure. That would make my question religious. I decided that I would ask him for advice.

As he finished his dinner and prepared to leave, I asked him if I might speak with him I told him of the hotel's spirits. He smiled and nodded. I explained to him about the invitation I was given to be hypnotized, because certain people believe that I can conjure.

"Don't let anyone hypnotize you! Of course you can conjure. It isn't as unique as you might think. We are all made in the Lord's image and we have the same powers as he has. Since we don't use them, we lose these wonderful abilities, usually early in life. Use this power for good things, Mildred."

"I am not aware of using it," I said rather weakly, while accepting the astonishing possibilities of this that both fascinates and frightens me.

Chapter 31: A Spirit Comes to Breakfast

It was Sunday, Memorial Day, 1981. Since it was 10:30 a.m., I had slept late, and as I walked into the café, Jan, who had been cooking since, 6 a.m. beckoned to me.

"We have a big problem, the stove isn't working!"

A glance at the large grill showed cold bacon, not sizzling.

"Turn the fire up!" I said. I stooped to look at the stove's gas jets, which were blazing.

"It is up as far as it will go. It was working just fine until fifteen minutes ago." Jan explained. "I think one of your little ghosts is warming his arse on the grill."

"Another phenomenon! What else doesn't work," I asked.

"The microwave," she answered, her voice sounding exasperated. "What are we going to do if I can't cook?"

"It might be an energy mass – it can't hurt anyone," I confided. "They float on the air so maybe it will get sucked up through the kitchen fan, or maybe it has already. Soon everything will be working again."

I left the kitchen. As I stepped into the café, I knew that I guessed wrong and my hope had gone up the kitchen fan.

The waitress was trying to get the coffee machines to work. Water was spewing everywhere out of openings that I didn't know coffee machines had. The water was not going in the direction of the glass pots which sat empty and hot in their proper places. The machine must have something covering the small hole that lets the coffee drip naturally, I checked both machines they looked normal. Could unseen fingers be covering the drip holes? Since the first pots of water had not gone in the right direction, the waitress had added another.

She helped me carry the now-heavily-sloshing machines to the sink area where we dumped out all the water from each. We plugged them in again, doing all that was necessary to make a good cup of coffee. They did not work, and once more spewed water.

Dana, our Sunday morning dish washer, brought the mop and bucket while adding another body to the cramped space behind the counter. Once more we carried the coffee machines to the sink area and left them to spew and drip.

"Milly, look at the milk machine – it's leaking," Dana whispered.

It was. Somehow, the handles, which have to be raised to get milk, by some mysterious means were allowing the milk to pour slowly into the shallow tray where normally a drinking glass would be.

I opened the small refrigerator that held the two five-gallon containers. I pulled up the two narrow hoses that allowed the milk to be drawn and I was able to pinch and clip them up into a non-dripping position. Meanwhile, as you might imagine, our customers were becoming restless.

"Isn't there anymore coffee?" someone moaned.

"Gad, what the heck is taking so long? Where the heck is out breakfast?" another person asked.

I eyed the crowd; wondering whether this group of Ione citizens and tourists would accept the information that I was about to tell them. I was sure that they would think that I was totally bonkers.

"Excuse me," I said aloud, while I continued to clap my hands and wait for their attention.

"You are all witnessing a phenomenon," I said. "We have one of the hotel's spirits in here. There is nothing to be frightened of; it is no more harmful that a soft breeze would be."

I was trying to get them to relax, although no one seemed uncomfortable, perhaps a bit apprehensive. One of our local men opened the front door wide and yelled, "Okay, George, get out of here, there must be some other place where you should be by now!"

All the local people laughed at that, knowing he was referring to the ghost that we might have identified. It did seem to be a humorous incident, until all of the catsup bottles laid down, as if being pushed over by a naughty child.

Some of the customers had seen enough. They smiled graciously as they left, some of them forgetting to stop at the cash register.

I suggested to the customers, "If you want to know when the spirit passes you, place a piece of napkin or tissue on the edge of the table and you will see it move. If you would like to feel the spirit as it passes, hold you bare arm out into the aisle."

"That was no soft breeze," said the man with the camera, "I sure hope I caught that little display on film."

We actually had to close the restaurant, informing those who insisted on entering that we had a dilemma and we could not cook, explaining that our electricity had gone goofy.

"Why is the café full of people?" one person said.

"If you are not cooking, what are they eating?" another questioned.

"They are finishing their breakfast that was served before everything went weird," I explained.

"I only want a short stack of pancakes – you can cook those on the grill. It is gas, isn't it?"

"Well come on in; we can only try."

The grill was still cold. Locals who, by now, had heard that something was happening at the hotel kept entering through the hall door. The crowd of people became a cozy group who had shared an experience. Yes, the pieces of paper moved, and some of them were blown onto the floor as the spirit passed. A spirit isn't a scary thing, just a curious thing.

At noon while the customers sauntered out, they were in a jovial mood. They occasionally looked around as if they were hoping to see another phenomenon.

At 1 p.m., Bill, Jan the cook, and I, entered the now-quiet café and the kitchen. I cleaned the milk machine and set it up to pour milk again. It performed perfectly as did all of the other appliances, except for one of the coffee machines. We had to throw that expensive piece of equipment away. From then on, we rented coffee machines; they were guaranteed to be replaced if they stopped working, even for spooky reasons.

Chapter 32: The Groaning Ghost

Old fashioned buildings are renowned for their lack of light fixtures. At night the dim loftiness of the hotel lobby caused some people to hesitate before attempting to navigate its crossing.

From the end of the front hall, lit by one lone bulb, to the start of the back hall which also had a single light fixture, nothing relieved the gloomy space between them. One other light under the staircase did its glaring best to shine on the wall phone while a light in the upper hall shone on the stair treads. The banisters cast striped shadows, even and straight, like prison bars on the walls and floor.

Chris had been out cooking on a long evening. Often times we felt exuberant, rather than tired, after our work shift. As he crossed the lobby on the way back from a trip to the garbage dumpster, he heard the hotel's front door squeak open, followed by female voices. One said, "We can walk quickly, I'm not afraid of the ghosts!"

"I'm not either, but I won't go in there unless we run!" the other voice replied.

In and out of the shadows they trotted. The two young women were so busy hanging onto each other for protection against the terror of a ghost that they walked right past Chris, who was standing in the kitchen doorways dressed in white.

When they left the lobby and walked down the back hall on their way to the ladies room, Chris, being a rascal, climbed into the well's surrounding box and crouched down to hide himself.

When he heard the mumble of voices as they returned to once again cross the lobby, he waited until they were abreast of his hiding place, then he gave a sickening groan and draped on limp arm over the top of the well box.

He could see them as he peeked over the top. He told me that the girls stopped and stood still, paralyzed with fear. They were experiencing exactly what they feared... the monster of their imaginations.

Their first reaction was to cling to each other. They seemed to explode into a frenzied type of movement not knowing which way to run each, impeding the other's escape. Looking into each other's face for a split second, they did not need, or wait for an explanation. Once dashed through the lobby, the other turned and ran down the hall and out the back door.

Chris sat down on top of the well's lid while he laughed. "I couldn't believe the disturbance that I had caused," he said. He also felt sorry for the girls, and was relieved that they had already visited the bathroom.

I'll bet those young ladies have often told that story of the groaning ghost in the hotel lobby.

Chapter 33: The Band

It was 2 p.m.; lunch was over, and the café was empty. I began to think about the yearly pool tournament between the champion men's team, which just happens to be the hotel team, and the champion woman's team from Vim's Club. The plans for a party to follow the game were my job. The food would be no problem, but hiring a band was a different matter.

The sudden realization that I had forgotten to look for a band caused me to cover my face with my hands and look toward the ceiling. I had a desperate emphatic expression when I said aloud, "Oh God, I need a band! And by tomorrow night!"

Because live music and free food cost money, we would need the crowd to stay after the pool game and drink if we were going to come out ahead financially.

First, though, I had to admit to Bill that I had forgotten to secure some music. Bill was our bartender today, and the business card file was beside the register. I knew that I couldn't sneak in there and snoop in the file without having to admit my blunder. The best thing to do was to ask his help. We both knew that getting a band on short notice was unheard of, and we needed one for tomorrow night. Before I could step across the hall, though, a local couple came in for a late lunch. I prepared it, and to a few minutes to gossip with them.

At 3 p.m. we watched as a motorcycle came to a stop in front of the hotel. The rider stood on the sidewalk for a moment while he surveyed the street of storefronts before walking into the café.

"How can I help you?" I asked.

"I'll have a cup of coffee, please!"

While I prepared his coffee, he turned and spoke to the couple.

"Excuse me," he said, "can you tell me about the two bars across the street. Are they rowdy? Do they use live music?"

The couple smiled. "My father owns Vim's Club," Don answered. "It's not rowdy, but you will have to ask him about the music."

"Hey," I said, "I'm the one who wants the music," my voice implying that he should know that.

The young man looked at me. "You do?"

I blushed. What made me say that?

He glanced around the café. "You want music in here?"

"No, silly, over there!" I gestured toward the hall door. "Come on, I'll show you, we have a saloon over there across the hall." He got up and followed me.

"Hey, honey," I called as we entered the saloon. "I've found a band for your tournament tomorrow night."

Bill gave me a surprised look. "Tomorrow night?" he repeated, as he offered his hand in welcome to the bike rider.

"I'm Bill."

"I'm Joe. But we couldn't play tomorrow night; we already have a gig!"

"We don't need a band until next Friday night," Bill said.

That news relieved my anxiety. "What about next Friday night?"

Joe was studying a small tablet. He looked up and said, "Yes we could do it then!"

"Great, our problem is solved."

"Wait a minute," Bill said. "Do you play country/western? That's the only music that we can use around here."

"That is the only kind we play. The band's name is Raw Hide."

"What do you charge?"

"$5.00 per man per hour – 6 men."

The band hired, I took Joe back into the café to finish his coffee. When Don and Trudy waved goodbye, they included Joe in their parting words, "Good luck! My dad is at the bar today if you want to ask him about playing over there."

As Joe sipped his coffee, I questioned him.

"What brought you to Ione today?"

"I don't know, the strangest thing happened. I was lying on the sofa, watching television. The idea flashed in my mind that I had got to come to Ione. I sat up and said to my mom, 'I've got to ride!' When she asked me where, I said, 'I've got to go to Ione.'"

"She looked a little puzzled and asked, 'Ione, do you mean that little town off of highway 88, below Jackson?'"

"'Yes, that's the one!' I told her."

"When she asked what was in Ione, I told her that I didn't know, I just had to go! So here I am."

As he finished the explanation, he shrugged and gestured with his hands, looking like he had just finished a tap dance routine.

For the first time, except for Bill and the priest, I was about to tell this stranger of my new realization! "I wished out loud for a band, so I must have conjured you!"

I laughed at the expression on his face. It was a mixture of 'you're kidding' and 'I hope you're kidding.'

Joe stood up and turned to face me. Standing behind the swivel chair, he twirled it and smiled. As he studied me I studied him. With his black wavy hair, dark eyes and handsome face he was certainly movie star material.

"Well, guess what? I heard you in Lodi! That's where I live." He shook his head, "I won't say that it was a voice that I heard, it was more like an idea with an urgency about it. My mother is not going to believe this."

"There aren't many people who will." I replied. "I did it and I'm finding it hard to believe that it happened."

I watched him as he patted his pockets.

"Oh no," he gasped, "I left my wallet on the television. I've got no money with me; I'd better drive carefully on the way home, since I don't have my driver's license."

"Don't worry about the money, the coffee is on me. After all, I did ask you to come up here. I can afford the 32 cents."

He continued to search the pockets of his coveralls as well as his jeans. In each pocket he found some coins. The final count came to exactly 32 cents. He put the coins on the counter and spread them apart and grinned as he plucked lint from among them.

"No bubble gum?" I teased.

He pointed toward the money, "Now that's incredible. What's your name?"

"I'm Milly; but I bet you thought that I was going to say Wanda Witch."

He laughed. "Goodbye, then. I'll see you next Friday. By the way, I'm not going to tell the other guys in the band how I secured this gig!"

During the following week, I was teased. I should not have told my employees about the strange way in which I had secured the band. They were convinced of a number of things.

One said, "They must be awful! A good band is usually booked up on a Friday night."

Mary added, "They are charging you such a low rate because they aren't worth any more than that."

"That's right," Eva said, "how much could their repertoire be worth – it only consists of ten tunes."

I didn't let them bother me. After all, I had met Joe; they had not. Each time I thought of the band, I looked toward the ceiling and asked, "Please, let them be good, if not terrific."

Friday finally arrived. The pool game was almost over, and the band had not arrived. At 9 o'clock we closed the café. When Eva locked the front door, she remarked, "Look at that fancy red jeep and silver trailer. It just parked in front of the hotel. Wow, look at all the cowboys!"

That remark brought the waitress and me running to the front door. There were cowboys all right, dressed in fringed buckskin jackets, black hats with silver braided hat bands, and black jeans. I stepped out onto the sidewalk.

"Hello Milly," Joe said, "I hope we're not late!"

"You are right on time. Everyone is waiting in the saloon."

I watched as the men pulled a rack on wheels from the trailer that held all of their instruments and speakers. The band set up at the back of the dance floor and started to play. With the first notes resounding through the large room I knew that this band was tops and very professional.

It was quite a party. I felt happy and shamefully smug. I glanced at the ceiling and said thank. Perhaps I should have looked into the mirror and said thanks to my reflection, but awe shucks, that would have been embarrassing.

Joe had not told the other band members about our mind connection. After the first break, when the band took a rest and came back to their instruments, the guitarist complained that someone had turned the knobs and he had to reset the guitar and amplifier. The second break, it happened again. The man became very upset. "What kind of a jerk would do such a thing?"

I took Joe aside and told him about our spirits who love switches and dials. That is when he decided to tell the other men. He also confessed to them how he had gotten this gig.

Thank goodness they all thought it was a funny, new experience and looked forward to any more weirdness.

The first thing we did to accommodate the guitarist was to put a bed spread over the electric console, guitar and amplifier when they stopped to rest.

By the way, the woman's team from Vim's Club lost the pool tournament that year.

That same evening we were expecting a family of four who had reserved our largest room. They were here to try to photograph our ghosts. They were friendly and full of good humor. The man took pictures with every kind of camera equipment. One camera had a special heat sensitive film. The results that he showed me were remarkable. The small camera, which looked like an ordinary Polaroid type, brought forth no ghostly image. He stood in the lobby just outside of the saloon door as we talked. He placed the camera on top of his head and took a picture of the balcony above us. The photo slid out of the camera, and we waited.

The man looked at his picture. "There he is," he whispered to me, as if he didn't want the spirit to hear.

I looked at the photo. It showed a red figure of a person bending over the balcony looking down, perhaps, watching the photographer. The figure showed nothing of face, hands or any other physical appendage.

The next day the family was all a-chatter as they told me of their unusual night, how they had played cards and how the table had lifted off of the floor.

They enjoyed a walk around Ione, and the most exciting thing about their outing was that the photographer got another remarkable picture. The mother and children were seated at the desk in the lobby. The man was standing halfway up the stairs to take their picture. As he sighted the camera, eye to viewer, a gray cloudy mist drifted across the stairway and he was able to photograph his family through it.

He told me he had a remarkable photo but couldn't show it to me because the film was the kind that needed to be developed. He did say that he hoped that it would become a magazine cover – which one he did not say. He did, however, promise to send me a copy.

This has got to be the most broken promise in the world, "I'll send you a copy." Oh well, I've seen, three spirits and two wonderful photographs. I did not receive any picture but perhaps they did not develop... that would not be the first time.

Chapter 34: Room #3

Doors that creaked open or slammed shut through no human effort were things we could shrug off by assuming they were caused by a draft or the settling of an old building. Drapes raised to ridiculous heights, as if they were waving, bed spreads being rumpled as we watched were things that we ignored. Water in the showers found running, lights that turned themselves on or off. We considered blaming human pranksters. What bothered us most was when the spirits wanted to play.

Our housekeeper Diane had the dust pan emptied onto the just-swept floor, as if some imp were teasing, waiting for a reaction. Once, she and I watched in disbelief as the broom became self-propelled for about ten seconds before slamming to the floor.

One morning I heard her talking, as if she were scolding a child. "I don't think you're funny! The door is open, so leave!"

Hearing this conversation, I climbed halfway up the stairs so that I could see into room #3 as she began to clean. My first thought was that perhaps one of our male residents was flirting with her, but I heard no other voice.

"Are you talking to one of our unseen friends?" I asked.

Diane came to the door. With her happy attitude and stocky figure, she could be described as being motherly.

"One of your friendly spirits," she said. "I know it's in here, because I had the feeling of walking through a spider web when I came in. The hair on my arms is still standing up. I told it that I would be in here for a while, in case it wanted privacy."

I came up the stairs to stand in the doorway with her and we made jokes about the spirits needing privacy.

"I would guess that they don't have to worry about safe sex," I said. I could tell by her expression that humorous idea had popped into her mind.

"Do you suppose that is where dust balls come from? Are they spirit babies?"

As we laughed the drapes did their silly thing by raising up and waving.

"Don't let that bother you. Think of it this way – the drapes on that window are now dust free."

Diane shrugged and trembled, like a cold chill had just engulfed her. "I think that I'll go and clean one of the rooms across the hall first." We walked away toward the linen room but couldn't help noticing that the door of room #3 was slowly swinging closed.

In 1981, I had a wonderful idea. For lunch each Friday I would make our daily special, Chinese food, because that is what I like to cook. It became popular with the locals and many customers came from other cities such as Jackson and Sutter Creek.

Our competition, in their restaurant across the street, also chose to make Chinese food. The only problem was they served it the day before we did, each Thursday. I felt sure that they were teasing me and I thought to tease them right back.

In 1981 they had a new idea. They had begun to make healthy cookies and sell them packaged in pretty tins. We would have to make a few cookies ourselves and advertise the fact. With a borrowed cookie gun and a sugar cookie recipe we made dozens. We advertised by painting a large sign to cover our front window. It read: *Homemade cookies, 50 cents a dozen.*

The great Ione cookie war lasted only two days and was talked about for a long time. No one cared that we served the same specials. They did make better cookies.

The front of the Hotel Ione

Chapter 35: The Goat to the Rescue

"Jerks," Patty said as she pushed through the swinging doors that divided the café from the kitchen. Her usually happy expression was now one of disgust. I was cooking, and I had just made three hamburgers. I had noticed that Patty had been making milkshakes, so I asked her, "What's the matter, mixer acting up again?" I knew that our old fashioned mixer would occasionally spray the waitress who had become inattentive.

"No, it's those goons out there," she gestured toward the café with her thumb, where the three young men sat, eating and laughing.

"They seem to be having a good time," I said.

"They may be, but I can't stand there rude remarks!"

"Rude? Not for long."

I walked out into the café and went behind the counter, where I poured myself a cup of coffee. I heard one of them remark, "Ow-ee, watch out, she sent mama out here!"

I smiled at them. "You are sure having a good time!" I said in a friendly manner.

"Not anymore," one said. "Send the waitress back out here!"

"She's busy, if you want anything else, I can get it for you."

"What we want, you can't give us!"

They roared with laughter. One of them blew a straw wrapper at me. I picked it up and in a friendly manner I asked, "Where are you from?"

"We're from Sacramento," one said, "But we already have mothers."

They laughed again. I knew that I couldn't handle these three – I needed help.

I left the café through the hall door and crossed to the small service window, which led into the saloon. I stuck my head through the opening.

"Hi," I called to Melanie, our bartender. When she approached, I asked if there were any men in there.

"Not a real one among them," Melanie answered. "What's going on, you got a problem in the café?" the only men sipping beer were two of our elderly patrons, who were usually inebriated. I told her what the problem was.

"Hey you two, watch the bar," she told the two men.

They glanced around, startled by the request, but ready to do the job.

I watched her as she stepped out the door and heard her speaking to someone. She was sending for a police officer.

I went back into the café and closed the hall door behind me. I leaned over the swinging door and said to Patty, "The police will be here in a few minutes." She was wringing a towel because the boys had spilled their water and had called for her to wipe it up. When she got close they had untied her apron strings and hummed the stripper music.

"Okay," I said, "The fun is over. We are closing, the police are coming in for their coffee break and it's time for you to leave. Have you given them their check?" I asked Patty.

"Yes," Patty answered. "The blonde one has it in his shirt pocket."

"The register is this way," I gestured to them.

They continued to lounge in the chairs; their smirking faces giving the impression that they felt in control.

The hall door was suddenly thrust open with such a great power that the table behind it was toppled. The opened doorway was filled with the 200-plus pounds of Rocky, one of the largest men in Ione. With his black hair, beard, and pretend anger, for a chilling moment, he looked like Ivan the terrible. Rocky also struggled to bring under control a charging, very large, black goat. Its menacing horns gleamed in the café lights as it strained against the taut chain.

"Is somebody in here bothering my waitress," Rocky bellowed.

The three men stood up in unison.

"It's okay fella, we don't want any trouble." The blonde man said.

"Oh yeah, when did you decide that? I hear you like to give trouble to nice ladies!" Rocky shouted. His voice, reverberating off the café walls and the fifteen foot ceilings, had an even more authoritative quality.

The trio stood up and threw three $5.00 bills on the table and walk backwards toward the front door.

"Is that enough money to cover their bill?" Rocky asked.

"Yep, that's enough." Patty said.

As one of them turned around to reach for the front door knob, the door opened and a police officer walked in.

"Everything all right in here?"

"There is no problem in here officer," the blonde man said as the trio left quickly.

We had a great laugh over the incident and thanked Rocky for being our hero. We followed Rocky and his goat outside, when he asked us if we wanted to see how well his goat obeyed. We gathered around the pickup truck for the demonstration.

173

"He loads real easy, watch... Up goat!" Rocky said as he jerked on the goat's chain. "Come on up-up," he repeated. The goat answered, sounding a bit like a duck with the hiccups. And it nibbled on the taillights.

The goat not obeying his command made Rocky decide to give it a boost, and he tossed it lightly into the truck bed.

"I told you it obeyed – see how easy it loads?" We all applauded the act, while the goat's chain was secured to the spare tire.

"Thanks, Rocky," Patty said. "I sure appreciate this."

Chapter 36: The Hooker's Ball

We were having a Halloween party – our third. We laughingly call it a "Hooker's Ball," a great name for a costume ball where everyone dresses up as a hooker or a pimp. It's a party in which a woman can play the glamorous prostitute, although sometimes they are, and a man can dress very flashy, as one would expect a pimp would, at least in the movies. This title for a party of this type is attributed to Margo St. James. I'm not sure about the reputations of those who attend her parties, but I am going to defend the reputations of every person who has ever attended one of our parties.

I had an invitation for an interview with a San Francisco radio talk show. I agreed to do the interview over the telephone – live, as they say. I assured the interviewer that I would not use foul language. I had to hang around the lobby phone as the time approached for the interview so I could keep any Ione residents from using it, as it was a pay phone as well as our business phone.

When it began, the interviewer asked, "What do you do in a haunted house on Halloween?"

"The ghost will have to entertain themselves," I blurted out, "because we are having a Hooker's Ball tonight."

Then I realized that I had told thousands of people, and some of the wildest partygoers in California, about our plans.

We wondered how many of those listeners might attend out party.

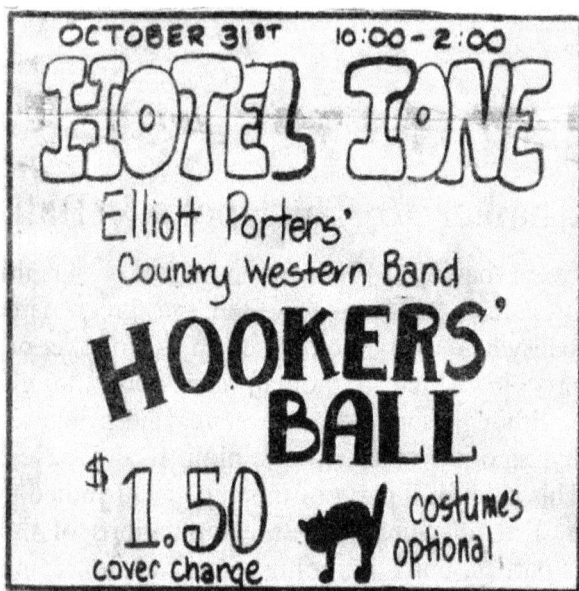

At 9 p.m. costumed, unrecognizable people were walking through the lobby greeting each other and trying to guess who was under that makeup, wig, and seductive attire. While I was upstairs putting on my costume, Bill looking terrific dressed in his best slacks, bright vest, sleeve garter and derby hat, was policing the lobby to keep kids from racing through it.

Two black men walked into the hotel carrying camera equipment.

"Can I help you?" Bill asked.

"Where is the Hooker's Ball being held? Would that be upstairs?"

"No, that would be in the saloon," Bill gestured toward the door.

"Our boss sent us to take pictures of the party."

"Who is your boss?"

"Margo St. James!"

"What has Margo St. James got to do with our party?" Bill asked.

"I guess that she heard about your party on the radio. She wanted to see if any of her friends were going to be here, and wanted pictures, just to look at the costumes."

"There is no possible way that I am going to let you take pictures of my guests. You are welcome to go into the saloon, watch the proceedings, relax and have a beer, but no pictures!"

"No problem; we'll tell Margo that you said no pictures."

Bill said, "Tell Ms. St. James that she is welcome to come up here to Ione any other time she would like to take pictures."

They didn't stay at the hotel but went across the street to Vim's for a cocktail.

When Bill told me the story, we laughed at the fact that Ms. St. James could be worried about competition from our little social event.

Our friend Bob was married to our waitress Mary. They arrived together for the Hooker's Ball, dressed as a couple. The difference with them was that Bob, who is the shorter of the two, was dressed as a woman, and Mary as a pimp. Although Mary wore a glued-on mustache, her feminine face and movements represented a type of effeminacy in a male that caused my masculine husband to feel uncomfortable. Just looking at this pretty, six foot tall young "man" would take understanding on his part.

Bill stood on the curb and watched them walking toward the hotel. Mary was taking long, exaggerated strides and had one hand stuck into her left jacket pocket. Her right hand was steering her high-heeled and be-wigged partner.

I joined Bill standing on the curb.

"Look at what your radio interview has brought to our party!" he whispered.

Before I could tell him that I recognized these two, Bill had accepted a hug from Bob, thinking that he was what he represented, but he recoiled from Mary who offered to shake hands as men do. Once Mary smiled at him, Bill recognized her and the charade was over.

Seven women arrived in a stretch limousine. Each of them was dressed exquisitely, with every fingernail gleaming, and their hair curled and placed perfectly. Some wore furs and others feathered boas. They sat together at one long table, which was placed next to the dance floor.

Two young women who Bill and I have all but adopted were there for the weekend – they have been visiting with us once a month for a year. Now they surprised me as they walked down the stairs dressed in frilly sleepwear. A risqué costume, for sure.

Back in the saloon we were continually surprised by the costumes of our guests. I had on a gold lamé housecoat and matching slacks, which I found at a flea market. That was not me at all, and I felt like hiding.

Bob approached us. "Now that you know who we are, I have to tell you about what happened over at Vim's Club. Two black men came in and ordered drinks. Then they went over to the piano and one of them began to play. The other stood next to the piano enjoying the music, as we all did."

"Two kids came in, one dressed like a Ku Klux Klan member. The other had his face blackened and wore a rope around his neck. The rope was being held by the hooded one."

"The piano playing stopped as this odd group stared at each other. The children didn't even say trick-or-treat. The boy wearing the hood took it off and smiled, trying to assure the real black men that he meant no disrespect. Then he raced out the door leaving his younger brother alone.

The piano player laughed at the joke. The embarrassing situation could not have been planned. The man standing by the piano gave the child a handful of candy.

"Thank you," the young man said, "I gotta go find my brother now." He was too young to realize what a blunder they had made.

Our party was a success. The music by Captain and Crew was great. The costumes were all winners. Vim closed his bar at midnight and he and Lois joined our party. They came dressed in Hawaiian clothes Lois wore a lei of condoms around her neck, keeping with the theme of our party.

We formed a conga line, and danced our way from the saloon through the lobby, under the stairs and down the long front hall to the sidewalk, and finally back into the saloon. The second time we did that, a police officer stopped us.

"Keep the party inside please," he said sternly.

We enclosed the officer in our line and he did the conga with us back inside.

Eddie, a great dancer, had a willing group of partners as the seven women obliged his polite request.

"Will you dance with me honey?"

He had a partner for every tune played. His stamina was remarkable, considering what he had imbibed over the course of the evening. The women never refused him a dance. As the last tune of the evening was being played, we noticed Eddie's secret for longevity on the dance floor. He was dancing with one foot and one arm while he hung onto the back of a chair with the other hand.

He never lost his balance and he thanked each woman for the dance. They were all gracious and never mentioned his strange method of Terpsichore.

Were these ladies some of Margo's friends? We never knew. At 2 o'clock, their chauffeur arrived for them and they scrambled into the long car and it moved slowly away.

We closed the saloon and sat around talking and sipping coffee and eating snacks. We were still visiting with each other when we noticed that shoes, wigs and glued-on mustaches were coming off. Then we used our most successful way to break up a party – we sang *Good Night Ladies…* that always works. Our only problem at that point was how to get up in three hours.

Bill's favorite holiday is Thanksgiving. In 1977, our first Thanksgiving Day in Ione, we celebrated the day alone. Our son and his family were in Korea, and our daughter in Washington State. We dined on steak in the coziness of our living room and then we sat out on the hotel's front balcony, watching the mostly-empty street.

The businesses were closed, except for Orville's and Vim's bars. We entertained ourselves by counting their customers. That is when Bill wondered if those people had already eaten a big Thanksgiving dinner, or were looking for some companions to celebrate with.

I wondered if their conversations would be about the way things used to be when they were kids, or when their family got together for a Thanksgiving reunion. We agreed to find out about those people and invite them to a big family style Thanksgiving dinner, feeding as many as we could and especially inviting those who might be spending the holiday alone.

The first part of November of 1978, we began talking of our plans with those whom we thought would be interested in coming to have Thanksgiving dinner with Bill and me. We would no longer be alone on that special day. That year we enjoyed having twenty-two guests join us in celebration.

As Thanksgiving of 1979 approached, we were asked if we were having another free dinner.

"Yes," we happily answered. "If you know someone who would like to come to dinner, tell them to be here before 3 o'clock." It is difficult to prepare a dinner not knowing how many guests will show up. We could only prepare it and when the food was gone, there would be nothing we could do about it.

Thanks to some very generous Ione citizens, and donations from our suppliers, the menu kept expanding. So did our guests. Not only in tummy-stretching, but in numbers. That year we had forty-seven guests.

Our fifth and last dinner was in 1982. It started with chips, dips and punch, in the saloon. We played the jukebox and danced. Since we owned the pool table the games were free. Those who dared took the stair slide.

Setting the table and cleanup were easy with so many happy volunteers. Here is our last menu which fed more than sixty guests: four dozen stuffed eggs/celery sticks, pickled beans, smoked oysters, Han, two turkeys, two geese, mashed potatoes, giblet gravy, creamed onions, sweet potatoes, cranberry sauce, hot rolls, pie, whipped cream or ice cream, and coffee.

Chapter 37: The Chanting Spirit

One of the waitresses went to Preston School to take a test for a job. As she walked to the entrance, she met a woman whom she recognized as one she had served at the hotel the day before. She greeted her and asked, "Are you waiting for your friend?"

"Yes!"

"It's pretty hot today, why aren't you at the hotel where it's cool? Didn't you stay there last night?"

"No, we didn't stay there, we were too scared. The man with the white beard gave our money back."

"What scared you?"

"Ah ha," she answered in her crisp Jamaican accent, "That place is haunted, I'll tell you!"

"If you saw something, you should go back to the hotel and tell Milly, she wants to know about anything spooky that has happened."

That is how I found out about the chanting spirit.

The two women had rented room #13. One of them had a friend who was incarcerated at Preston. She left her friend, the Jamaican woman, at the hotel, to take a nap on the warm afternoon. Not understanding that the air conditioner cools the room if the door is kept closed, she tried to get comfortable by leaving the door open.

As she thumbed leisurely through a magazine, the sound of someone humming made her pay more attention to the sound than to the magazine. As the sound became louder, she stepped into the hall to listen. She became aware that it was not humming, but chanting. She quietly listened at the door of room #14, and then stood in front of room #12, hoping no one would come out; these rooms were quiet.

She told me that as she sat on the edge of the bed, the chanting became louder, as if a person was approaching her and speaking in a deep masculine voice. The language sounded like it might have been in African or Aborigine language.

She tried to imitate the sound.

"Hum-mm-nah, Hum-mm-nah! Like that," she said. Her face looked like she expected me to have an answer to this strangeness. I had no such information.

I watched her as she waved her expressive hands around while she described what had happened to her.

"I was wearing an off-shoulder dress. As the humming sound grew louder, I felt a hand caress my bare right shoulder. I was not afraid of spirit, oh no, I was willing to experience the phenomenon. His chanting stopped and it was very quiet. I began to feel nervous like I was waiting for something even more peculiar to happen. The hair on the back of my neck moved, then I felt my hair being softly and lovingly brushed away from the right side of my face. The hand again touched my shoulder, and then quickly it dropped to the low front of my dress. Hey!" I shouted.

"I thought of how stupid I must look and how dumb I was acting. I thought that I must be more tired than I had realized, and I became determined to just lie down and forget about it. The bed felt good and I would have dozed, but as soon as I got comfortable, the chanting began again."

"Then can you believe it, the pest tried to cop a feel! He ran his soft hand, or something, up my leg to here!" she pointed to her thigh. "That's it," I said. "I give up! You can have this room."

She then ran down the stairs and into the café where she asked for ice water, and then rather nervously asked for a cigarette.

"Are you all right?" the waitress asked.

"Yes I'm fine, never better, I just need a smoke."

When her friend returned, she met her in the lobby and whispered, "This place is haunted. I just got felt on my chest and up my leg, by a ghost or something."

"Sure you did," said Sharon, her doubtful friend.

"Come upstairs, I have closed the door, so maybe it is still there. It even chants."

"Chants?" her friend repeated, as they raced up the stairs.

"Just lie on the bed, close your eyes and wait."

The chanting began quietly. "Hum-mm-nah."

Sharon opened one eye, "I hear it," she whispered, "I think it's sneaking up on me."

She was wearing a pair of wide-legged cotton slacks, and she was barefoot. Her shirt was tied in a bow at the waist.

"As I watched Sharon lying there, the chant continued. She wiggled her foot, as if she were being tickled."

"Oh, oh," Sharon said, as she raised her head up from the pillow and we both looked in the direction of her right foot. She opened her mouth as if she were trying to bear the mysterious attempt at seduction, her pants leg moving up. "I wonder how far he will go. I believe that this one is not completely dead!"

When her pants leg rumpled up to her knee, Sharon gave a kick of her leg, and jumped off of the bed.

"Let's get out of here, maybe we can get our money back, since we didn't use the bed or the towels!"

"We told the man in the bar that we had an opportunity to stay with friend, and he gave us back the money."

"There is the story. We could not have slept in that room last night. We were worried about being in the dark with that one."

After she finished her story, I said, "I am glad that you came back to tell me the story of your spooky incident, and I am sorry if you were disturbed by it. I am sure that I could rent that room to lonely women!"

Chapter 38: The Scarf

Sherry and her husband came to visit the hotel to see for themselves this place with mysterious happenings.

"We read about it in the *Sacramento Bee*!" she said. "Would it be possible to rent room #4? We are anxious to experience the ghost!"

"Today must be your lucky day; the room is available. But, I must tell you, that you may be disappointed when it comes to seeing a ghost or a spirit, because George the ghost has not, to my knowledge, bothered a man and a woman who have shared the room. Only men who have been alone."

"We want to sleep there anyway!"

The next morning, Sherry told me this story. "During the night the door opened and before one of us could jump from the bed and to close it, a woman was standing in the opening. With light from the hallway behind her, we couldn't see her face but we could see that she was wearing a long dress of dark material and a bonnet."

Sherry continued, "I turned on the bed-side lamp. Its soft glow did little but reflect on the walls and ceiling. Her arms were outstretched in a pleading gesture, her words were softly spoken: 'Help my baby! A fire is burning!' We leapt from the bed and rushed toward the woman. In the mere seconds that it took to reach the door, the woman was gone, and the door was still solidly closed and locked. Flicking on the room's overhead light and opening the door, we viewed an empty hallway."

Were they thrilled? I believe that they were. When I asked her, she didn't hesitate to reply.

"You bet were thrilled! It was a once in a lifetime experience."

Do you think that Sherry and her husband saw the ghost of Mary Phelps, the pillar of smoke that I saw in the dining room in 1977? I do; the only difference is that this time, Mary had accumulated enough energy to appear as a more visible spirit.

We found out that Sherry was a country western singer, and signed her up for performance the next weekend, the first of many.

Sherry and Bud

One of Ione's older couples drove to Main Street twice a day for meals. Because they were elderly, I was drawn to them and found them to be very special people. Their attention to each other went beyond the usual door opening or chair holding. She would ask him if his food were hot enough, and he would ask her if the air conditioner was bothering her. If she felt chilly he would drape his jacket around her shoulders. They flirted with each other and she told him things that made him laugh. If he teased her, telling her that the bread pudding would make her fat, she would reach across the table and muss up his handsome white beard.

One afternoon they arrived early for an anniversary dinner.

"How long have you been married?" I asked, expecting them to say many years.

"Guess!" he asked.

I was thinking in the fifty year range, but I said, "Forty years."

"Oh no, much less, only twenty years! We look like this because marriage has been hard on us; we are only forty years old!"

We laughed at her joke, and he said, "That woman is a rascal!"

One day as he sat reading the paper while she toyed with her food, she waved to me as if to get my attention. Because she had been ill, he never let her take a step without his steadying hand on her arm.

I waved, sending back what I thought to be just a friendly greeting.

She stood up and stepped forward. She was already three feet from the service window before he realized what she was doing. I was so amazed at seeing her walk unaided that it took me a few seconds to shift into gear and rush to her side.

"Milly," she said, "I saw him! The little boy ghost. He smiled at me!"

"How did you know he was a ghost?"

"Because he was such a quiet little boy and I could see right through him. He went out through that door." She pointed toward the hall door.

I walked her back to her chair.

"Are you okay, honey?" he asked.

"I must be better than ever," she said, "I saw a ghost and I didn't faint."

I am still trying to find out just what is happening at the hotel. What has brought these spirits, or awakened them? Thank goodness no one has been hurt and only a few guests have been disturbed by them. If these beings were going to hurt us, surely it would have happened by now.

Our ghostly situation was described in the *Sacramento Magazine*, for Oct. 1981. A lengthy article titled, "Haunted Houses, Haunted Minds." In it, the author, Betty Johannsen wonders if psychometry or psychokinesis might be the cause for our spirits.

Since I promised myself that I would find out as much as I could about this phenomenon, I went right to the dictionary. Webster's Twentieth Century, Copyright. 1940.

Psychometry: Measurement of time consumed in mental operations.

Psychokinesis: explosive cerebral action due to defective inhibition.

Inhibition: in psychology and psychiatry, the checking or arrest of an impulse, desire or action by an opposing impulse, desire or action.

Matter: stuff of which anything is composed. Substance that may be felt weighed or seen. Has physical properties, as wood, stone, glass, water, air and smoke.

Mass: the sum of all the material particles of a body.

One afternoon I met two couples standing in the lobby, they were gazing up the stairs at the painting of the unicorn in the poppy field.

"I like that painting!" the older man said.

"That's my favorite also! Welcome to the Hotel Ione."

The older woman picked up on my play-on-words and smiled.

"Hi," I said, "I'm Milly, and my husband and I own it!"

They introduced themselves, telling me that they were from Sacramento and just out for a day's ride: Father, Mother, Daughter, and Son-in Law.

I answered their questions about the painting and took them upstairs. I showed them some of the rooms ending in room #4, as I told them about George and his seventy appearances. They were wonderfully attentive and it was nice to talk to people who are interested in the stories. I told them how fond I had become of George, Mary and the sweet-faced little boy. I didn't know how much more they would want to hear, but I rushed on.

"After living among the spirits for several years, I have come up with a theory of my own. Would you like to hear it?"

"Yes we would!"

"When a person dies, the body is taken away but the energy of that human, and the aura which surrounded the living body, stays in the room until it can gather energy from another source. Renewing their energy allows them to move about."

"What source?" the older man asked. "This is so interesting!"

"First of all I must explain to you what Webster's Dictionary says about the aura."

Aura: Literally, a breeze or a gently current of air. But technically denotes any subtle invisible fluid supposed to flow from the body. In a painting, and illuminations surrounding a holy person such as Christ.

190

I continued to talk. "All living things exude energy, aura, some people say that they can still see aura and even tell you what color yours is! Most people cannot see aura but here in the hotel we have found out that it is possible for some people to feel it."

"For example, have you ever visited with an older person, one who is frail or ill, they will always tell you that they feel so much better when you visit them. Sure they do, for two reasons. Because they are usually lonesome and we all need attention and affection, but the other reason they feel better is because you probably hugged them. They were probably weaker than you, so when you did that, they stole a piece of your aura. The next day you may feel more tired than usual, not being aware of the hole that you now have in your aura. You can fix that hole by hugging a child or your dog, both have plenty of energy to share. Or you may be lucky and sit with you back against a tree. The trees aura is very strong, that is why you will always feel good after a walk in the woods. The tree's aura has revitalized you."

I paused to see if they still seemed interested. They did, so I continued. "We here at the hotel, by our presence, have revitalized the spirits. I believe that because after years of idleness the hotel itself has been brought back to life. With so many people living, working and visiting, we have been able to give these spirits enough energy to appear. Sometimes as they looked when they were living, a ghost, and sometimes only as a floating mass, a spirit, with energy to tip things over, fluff our hair, pinch our bottom or give, a gently refreshing breeze. I sure can't explain how clothing is affected, but so far I have not seen any nude ghosts. Maybe that's why we don't see the sprits – they're nude in their energy mass form."

"Wonderful," the older man said, goading me to tell them more.

"The aura when it floats is called an energy mass. This is information I got from one of our guests. I am repeating it, not knowing if it is true. This energy mass cannot pass through the thick walls of old buildings and that is why ghosts are found in castles."

"It has something to do with physics, wave mechanics, speed of light and gravity. I have no knowledge of things like that; I can only give my theory. I do like the idea that we can hang around after death and be with the people we love, maybe read over their shoulder. I think that the secret must be to die at home. That way when your spirit leaves your body it will already be where it wants to be!"

"Until someone opens a window," said the son-in-law.

We all laughed at that. Our minds were reeling with the humor and the possibilities of being able to stay home after death, and watch what is happening to our loved ones as they live on.

"Hey, that's a hoot, Milly. I like your theory; it sure sounds good to me."

"Wait until you hear this theory," I teased. "Albert Einstein believed that our streets and sidewalks are crowded with energy masses. They could rise to the atmosphere, to the hemisphere and to the ionosphere. They were most likely the reason for the thumping sounds which were heard through the earliest radio receivers."

"Someday we will find out," the older woman said.

We shook hands as they said goodbye. The older man took my hand and said the most flattering thing "I am so glad we came here today. You are a special person Milly. We will plan on a return visit." When he withdrew his hand from mine he left a folded $10.00 bill.

"I don't charge for telling stories."

"Keep it," he insisted. "I want you to have it. You have made our day and deserve a reward. Buy yourself something pretty."

Three months later, I was surprised to find the same people once more in the lobby.

"Hello," the older woman said, "do you remember us?"

"Hello, yes of course I do, where is the mister?" I asked, meaning the older man. "Is he down the hall?" I nodded toward the restrooms.

"No," she took a deep breath and held it as she said, "he died!"

This news overwhelmed me.

"Was it an accident?" I asked as I sat down.

"When we were here, we knew that he was dying," she explained. "But he didn't want you to know. He got such a big kick out of your spirit talk because he had a secret. He told many of our friends about you and the hotel. We wanted you to know that because of your stories, he asked to die at home. We have all felt his presence since his death."

I was stunned into silence. How sweet of them to want to share this personal part of their lives with me.

"Thank you," the older woman said. She sat down next to me and gave me a motherly embrace.

I told them that he had given me the $10.00, and that I had purchased a fine scarf. "When I wear it, I will think of you all."

Chapter 39: Childhood Dreams

If you had visited the hotel, or come to one of our parties, you may have met and enjoyed our special entertainers.

Dennis, a talented pianist, was able to transform any ordinary evening into a happy time with a sing-along or an impromptu talent show. He could even accompany me, as I often felt like entertaining; while I felt like Sophie Tucker, I was hoping to sound like Linda Ronstadt. Dennis played the piano each weekend at the National Hotel in Jackson.

Red, who played the guitar and sang the old-style cowboy songs was such a pleasure to hear. He surprised us when he began to yodel with the clearest high notes that I have ever heard. His appearances brought a different crowd both in dress and in attitude. The last I heard of him, he was in Las Vegas.

Sherry, a pretty blonde, played guitar and sang country western songs, interspersed with some of the songs which she had written. She has made several recordings and is well on her way to a singing career.

Captain's Crew, our own Ione band, was always a sensation for smooth dancing. Bud, another Ione citizen, was a bass player par excellence and we were always honored to have him arrive and add his talented presence.

Mark, without notes or written composition, is an extemporaneous jazz pianist, who has a way with the 88 keys.

No music affects me like that of slow blues being played on an old piano in a quiet and dimly-lit saloon.

Our jukebox was filled with recordings of popular music, thanks to our younger customers. When John Travolta danced in the movie *Saturday Night Fever*, not only was the record *Staying Alive* popular in the saloon, but several of our bartenders, waitresses and I took lessons from a local teacher. With swaying hips and flailing arms, we filled the dance floor, no partner needed. Disco was a lonesome dance, but the exercise sure left you feeling great.

On quiet evenings, with ten people or less in the saloon, it was great fun to pass a microphone along the bar and coax each person to tell a joke. All the jokes got either a laugh or a groan. Both of these sounds, amplified by a few decibels, brought in more business.

Once you started you can surprise yourself by remembering a joke which you first heard in grade school. It is amazing what useless stuff our memory contains.

Once a year we hired the East Bay Banjo Blub from Concord California. With forty banjos in the saloon it was the loudest music, but it has such a happy sound that the volume was never a problem. Their special interest is handicapped children and they donate all of their proceeds to various organizations.

We did have one other singer who came to the hotel a few times a year. Not to entertain, but to sleep. After visiting the bars across the street, he was too intoxicated to drive home. We have always been glad that he thought of our establishment. He caused no problem until he lay down. He would then begin to sing at the top of his voice, which was considerable. I was certainly pleased with his baritone voice; he had perfect pitch and was always in tune. However I had never heard such volume come from anyone's throat. Ethel Merman would have been envious of it. There were two rooms between us, and I could still hear every word.

Because I could not sleep and I was sure he was disturbing our other guests at the hour of 2 a.m., I would put on my blue robe and walk down the hall to knock on his door. He was asleep and unaware that he was singing, so it took a long time before he answered.

"Please stop singing – you are disturbing the other guests!" I said, after my insistent knocking was answered by "Huh?"

"I'm sorry," came his answer.

As soon as I got back into bed, he would begin to sing again. It wasn't only that he was singing so loudly that drove me nuts, it was that he would forge the words, and begin a new song. This was maddening for a singer who prided herself on remembering the words to songs. I would feel compelled to finish the song, singing it silently in my mind. Only my pillow pulled over my ears helped.

I guess he only sang during his first attempts at sleep because after about an hour he would become quiet. In the morning he would be gone, taking his vast repertoire of unsung melodies safely home.

One night as I was finishing my last kitchen chores, I heard a woman's voice singing. I checked to see if the radio had been left on. It wasn't. I stepped into the hall and didn't hear it out there – the voice was only in the café, and kitchen, but not especially louder in either room. The melody was wonderful and as the song was repeated I grabbed a pencil and the cardboard back from a composition school tablet. When I had finished writing the words, I sang along with the voice until it stopped.

I sang the song out loud, reading the words that I had scribbled, afraid that I might forget the tune. I had to tell Bill about it! I locked the kitchen door and dashed up the stairs to our apartment.

"You'll never guess what just happened," I blurted out, exhausted and out of breath after running up the stairs. "I hate to admit it, but I'm hearing voices. I guess that's bad."

"What did you hear?"

"Someone sang a song to me," I gasped, "and I wrote down the words."

"Who?" he asked.

"I don't know," I answered, as I watched a look of puzzlement come over his face.

As my breathing returned to normal, I explained once more about the strange happening.

"It was so amazing! After I had written the words, the song was repeated and I was able to sing along with her voice. I felt that she wanted to give me the gift of her song. I'm only sorry that I was unable to record it."

"Can you sing it for me?"

"I'll try!"

When I was just a little child, a year or two ago
I dreamed of things I couldn't be
Of things I didn't know
I dreamed of flying all around
Skimming along the ground
Over the hills and plains, and then
I chased my shadow again.
I saw tiny creatures, looking at me
Fields full of poppies, a bright orange sea,
Over the lake, a reflection of me
Over the ground again.
Oh childhood dreams, where have you gone
I can no longer fly
The unicorn I'll see no more
No castles in the sky.
Now that I am older, I dream a different way

I dream that I'm the very best, at all I do and say
I dream of things I can't possess,
Of friends I'll see no more
I await a dream of love, then I won't fly
I'll soar.

"That is a pretty song! Really beautiful words," Bill commented.

I was so afraid that I would forget the melody that I could not sleep, and I kept practicing it in my head.

The next morning I was anxious for Dennis the pianist to arrive. As he sipped his coffee, I explained the incident and showed him the words to the song. I asked him if he could help me put the melody into written notes. I really thought that if I could sing it, he could write down the notes. His advice put me to work.

"Go to the music store and buy a citation manuscript book. It has pages of printed lines that you will have to write the music notes on."

"I can't write music; all I know I learned when I was five years old. E-G-B-D-F, Every Good Boy Does Fine, are the names of the lines and F-A-C-E are the names of the spaces."

"I can't possibly help you until you get the tune out of your head and onto paper. You could leave it out where the spirits may find it, and maybe they will write down the note for you. I've heard of spirit writing," Dennis quipped.

We left two off-duty waitresses, who took over the waitressing duties in our absence, and who promised to call me if there were any requests for breakfast.

Jodie said that she could play the piano a little. That was an understatement; she played well.

When she played the melody, with one hand, I felt such a relief. I no longer had to be afraid of forgetting the melody and my carefully-written music could be played.

I had no idea as to how to write the base notes, so there were none. Jodi began to add some base notes of her choosing, and we began to sing. When we finished, the beauty of the song overwhelmed us, and we both had tears in our eyes.

When Dennis arrived, he played the song with his flowing style. The music resounded through the empty saloon. I thought of the spirit who had given me the song and I hoped that she was pleased.

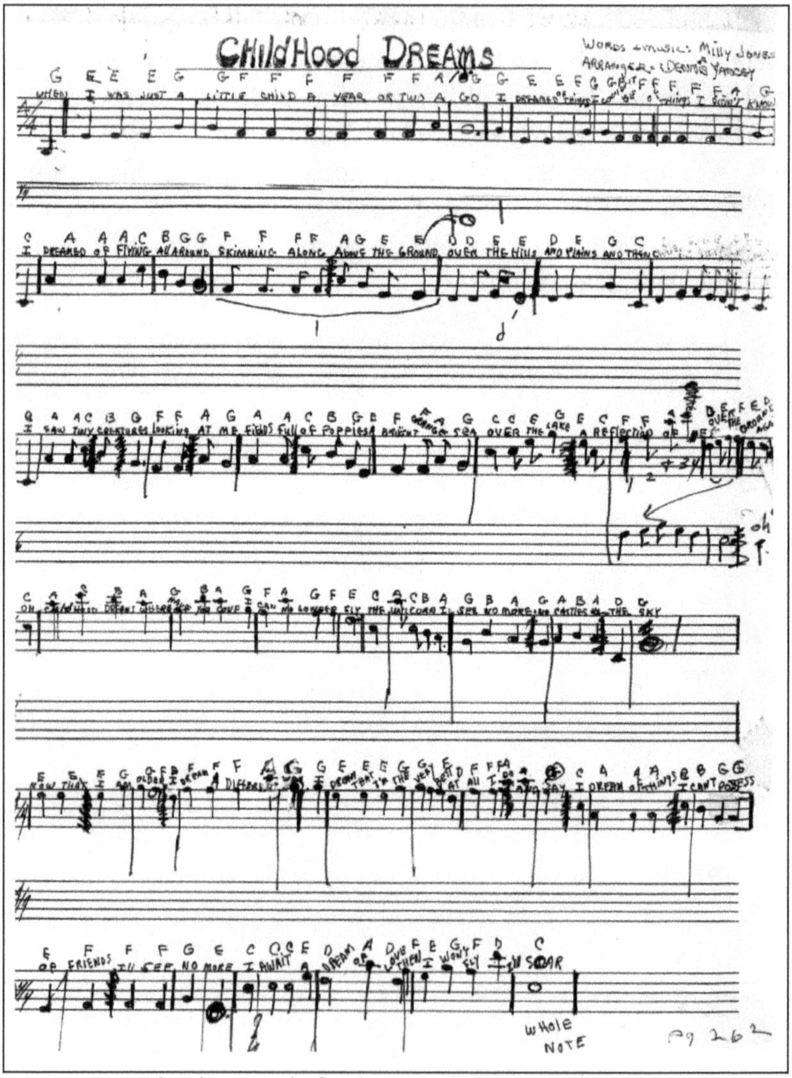

The sheet music for the song that was sung to me

Chapter 40: Tragedy

By 1983, two of the sand plants closed and construction on Rancho Seco, the atomic energy plant, was just about complete. Once it started functioning, fewer employees would be needed than during the construction phase. All of those hundreds of people left the area to work at another atomic energy plant.

The food business became very popular in Ione. The law that each bar must serve hot or cold food to ward off public drunkenness brought an influx of pizza ovens, popcorn machines, microwaves and hotdog roasters.

Ione's drive-in reopened. The donut shop served sandwiches. There was a Mexican restaurant, and two sandwich shops. Also, Preston School and the fire academy had cafeterias. With so few customers divided among us, there was just enough income to cover wages and costs. That is when we rented out the café, and got out of the food business.

Bill decided that after six years of bartending he would rather do something else. He went to work at the Ione Brickyard, while I played at bartending.

Early in 1984 Bill broke his back. Because he needed my attention, our friend Morgan took over the hotel and saloon. He devoted himself to operating it the way we would. After a month of dividing my time between Bill's care at home and checking on things at the hotel, it became clear that the best thing to do was to sell the hotel. We did so on July 1, 1984.

About the ruffled edged glass plates that kept appearing mysteriously… although I had only asked for a dozen, by 1980 we had received fourteen and broke two. Before we sold the hotel those two had been mysteriously replaced.

When we moved from the hotel, I brought the dishes with me and my mother's buffet that we had used as a part of the hotel dining room furniture. A year later I was shocked to find that we now had nineteen plates. The difference being, that five of them were tiny, ice cream scoop size.

I said to Bill, "There is only five, what can I do with five?" Then I scolded toward the ceiling, as I had so many years ago, "You know how I hate uneven numbers; where is the sixth one?"

Bill laughed at me. "Good try, but this is no longer the spirited hotel. It won't work this time."

"You are probably right," I said, "but nothing ventured, nothing gained."

A month later we had friends staying or dinner and since they already knew the story about the mysterious dishes I had to show them the little ones.

"How about that… in the darkness of the buffet, the big ones have presented us with quintuplets."

Wrong – the sixth one had arrived.

On Father's Day, 1988, Jim and Pam, whom I met one evening as they sat on the hotel's staircase, had been discussing the spider's webs that continuously draped themselves in the skylight.

"We like the decorations," she said.

"Those are sheer curtains that I don't have to iron."

"And those guests are quieter."

And so it went, quip after quip until we had become friends. For years they spent time at the hotel while visiting our

Amador county and its attractions, even filling in as a waitress or a bartender on occasion.

Today being Father's Day, they had come to take Bill and me out for breakfast.

At the Buena Vista restaurant, three miles from Ione, a local farmer walked in and said, "The hotel's on fire."

"The one I own?" Bill asked.

"Yeah, it's burning like crazy! They will never put that one out – it's gone."

"No," I said, not wanting to believe this bulletin of tragedy. While tears filled my eyes, I looked at Pam and her hands were covering her face.

When we arrived in Ione, we joined the mass of onlookers who stood along Main Street watching quietly. As we passed, friends stepped forward to hug us, then to turn quickly away, not wanting to see our tears.

Even though we had sold the hotel four years earlier, our love for the old building had brought us there to watch and to worry along with the new owners.

The building built of cement blocks was burning on the inside, like a box with a thin lid. The old and heavily-varnished woodwork exploded, helping the hungry fire devour all that the flames touched. The pungent smoke soon found our nostrils, making us realize how close we were standing.

A fire makes a loud noise. It was an indescribable sound because there is nothing in my memory to compare it to. We could hear window glass breaking, the old and wavy ones. The chopping sound of the fire axe on the walls and floors. The roar of the flames, and loudest of all the noise of water being forced from pressure hoses onto the metal roof.

Each sound could be singled out, like listening for the oboe's part in an orchestra.

Flames escaped from the now-broken glass of the eight windows and a door that were across the upper front of the hotel. Each of them had opened onto the graceful balcony.

One of the hotel residents collected black powder weapons. So he had a supply of gunpowder on hand. When the fire found its way into his room, the black powder exploded causing a different sound. It was a deep boom, whose location could not be discovered until a spectacular burst of black smoke followed by a shower of tiny shards of wood, glass and metal sent those people who were standing in the street running for safety.

The fire was burning rapidly, from the front of the hotel to the rear. From the street I could see where it was as it presented itself in each window. The curtains would flame. Then the wooden window frames blazed and the glass crackled before it burst and melted.

Our concern was for the guests, and we were jubilant to hear that everyone had escaped safely.

Now my thoughts were for the staircase which I loved. This handmade beauty standing in the center of the hotel had been protected for seventy-eight years by the skylight. Soon I was sure of its fate; smoke billowed from the open skylight, like it was coming from a gigantic chimney.

I turned away to look into the sad faces of the present owners. They put up their hands, gesturing the hopelessness that we all felt. They had devoted more time doing physical labor to renovate the hotel than even they were willing to speak about. It was the same love of a building that had made Bill and me reluctant to change its style.

People milled around asking how the fire started. We were told that children playing with a cigarette lighter had started it.

When the hotel was built, President Taft was in the White House. Hailey's comet was on its way and woman's dresses swept the dust from the raised platform that served as a stage stop and hotel entrance. Now that entrance was burning. The front porch collapsed upon itself, and then it fell to the sidewalk.

More bright fire trucks arrived. Their chrome glittering in the sunlight, seemed out of place in the smoky atmosphere. Their sirens seemed to scream "We're here, you're saved!"

Unfortunately, the hotel was not saved. What was left of its walls now stood sadly among the rubble, looking like a jack-o-lantern a week after Halloween, with empty eyes and a hollow center.

I had never worked so hard, nor laughed as much as I did while learning to be a cook, bartender, housekeeper, bookkeeper, party arranger and diplomat.

Bill and I will never forget the love and loyalty we felt from our employees and guests. As for the spirits and the ghosts, we were surprised and curious rather than frightened.

A phone call from an Ione citizen told me to go and buy the local paper.

"The picture of the hotel on fire is remarkable," Jim told me. "I believe it shows faces of the ghosts in the smoke."

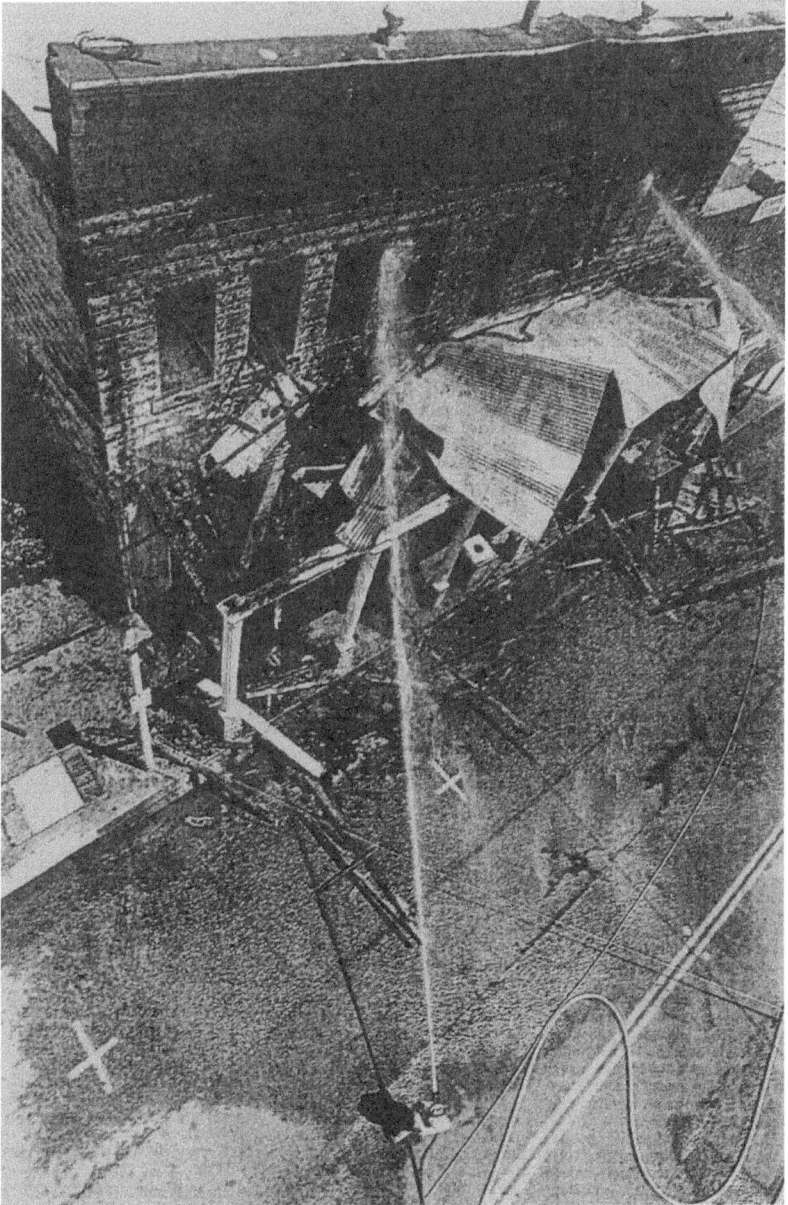

Hotel Ione History & Rebirth

Over its life, the Hotel Ione has seen many seasons – fires that ravaged it, loving owners who rebuilt it, and various periods of remodeling and restoration. It has operated under different names over those years. Its guests have arrived on a stagecoach, on horseback, and of course, on motorcycles and in automobiles. Through it all, the grand old lady of Ione, California has persevered.

The original **Union Hotel** located on the property had a bar, a restaurant, and 25 rooms. There was a stagecoach stop and stable on the south side of the building. It burned around 1890.

Next came the **Ione Hotel**; Guiseppi and Rosa Tonzi bought the lot and built a small hotel of wood. It had gas lights and a woodstove. A bakery was at the back of the building. The Ione Hotel burned in 1908.

The same owners, Guiseppi and Rosa Tonzi, re-built in 1910 and opened the **Golden Star Hotel**. Guiseppi designed and built the building, including the fancy woodwork and stair spindles turned on a treadle lathe. Cement blocks for the exterior walls were hauled into place by means of a pulley system and horse power. It was sold to the Stacy Family in 1971 and renamed the **Stacy Inn**. In 1977, the hotel was sold to Bill and Milly Jones, who renamed it the **Ione Hotel**. The hotel was sold in 1984, and tragically burned in 1988.

Today the new owners have rebuilt the **Hotel Ione** with extensive renovations, including a mahogany staircase and private bathrooms for every guestroom. The hotel is once again fulfilling its destiny by serving visitors to the city of Ione, California.

Hotel Ione Recipes

In the pages that follow are several of the recipes that our customers requested.

Phyllis' Bread Pudding Rum Sauce

This rum sauce is a perfect topping for the bread pudding recipe that is on the next page.

2 cubes of butter or margarine
2 cups powdered sugar
1 can evaporated milk
1/3 bottle of rum flavoring

Melt butter or margarine in the top of a double boiler. Stir in the sugar until dissolved and add the can of milk. Reduce heat to simmer and cook for 25 minutes, or until sauce coats the back of a spoon. Remove from heat and stir in the flavoring.

This sauce will separate when stored in the refrigerator. Just reheat, and stir to make it smooth again. It will keep well for a week. It is also good on sponge cake.

Hotel Ione Bread Pudding

The ten loaves of bread that we used every day for sandwiches left us a surplus of ends or heels. It was toasted and used for crumbs or made into bread pudding. Here is a smaller version. It is my grandmother's bread pudding recipe, which is delicious when served with Phyllis' recipe for rum sauce

5 slices of bread
3 Tbl of butter or margarine
½ cup white sugar
2 Tbl cinnamon
1/3 cup raisins
3 eggs slightly beaten (if you want it lighter, whip egg whites and fold them in)
1 tsp vanilla
¼ tsp salt
2 ½ cup warm milk
½ tsp baking powder

Heat the oven to 350 degrees F. Grease 1 ½ quart casserole. Toast bread (lightly) and spread with butter. Cut bread into small pieces. Place into a large bowl and add all other ingredients. Stir well, wetting all the bred pieces. Pour into greased casserole; sprinkle with more cinnamon. Set casserole into shallow pan, with water about an inch deep. Bake 65 minutes or until a knife stuck into the center comes out clean. This Bread Pudding re-heats well in the microwave.

White country gravy (made with sausage)

We served this over hot biscuits, split and buttered.

½ package skinless pork storage (4 sausages)
2 Tbsp flour
2 cups cold milk
1/8 tsp garlic powder
1/8 tsp onion powder
Salt and white pepper to taste.

Lightly brown the sausage until pink disappears, because you want the gravy to be white.

Break up the sausage as they fry using a fork or a whip. Add the flour and stir until it is absorbed by the grease. Pour in the milk, reduce the heat and stir until thickened.

Frittata

A frittata is a cross between an omelet and a quiche. It is delicious hot as an addition to a dinner, or served cold as a canapé.

4 eggs, separated
2 medium zucchini (shredded)
¼ lb American cheese (shredded)
½ a medium sized onion (shredded)
¾ tsp salt
½ tsp white pepper
½ tsp onion powder
½ tsp garlic powder

Beat egg whites very stiff. In another bowl whip egg yolks until they are foamy. Add all other ingredients, stirring until all is coated with the yolks.

Fold in the egg whites. Pour into greased 8x8 inch pan, bake for 45 to 50 minutes, or until frittata pulls away from the sides of the pan.

To serve cold I prefer it a bit firmer. This allows it to be picked up with the fingers and not break apart.

To the above recipe I add:
½ cup of flour
1 tsp of baking powder

Shrimp Scampi

This recipe for scampi is expensive, but if you are going to spend all that money on prawns you might as well spend some on a cube of butter. Margarine, no matter how wonderful, will not make a rich, flavored sauce. We served five large prawns for each order, so this recipe is for two people.

10 prawns
3 Tbsp butter
1 Tbsp oil
1 large clove of garlic, stuck onto a toothpick
1/8 tsp salt
1/8 tsp onion powder
2 tsp chopped parsley
2 tsp tarragon leaves (crushed)
2 Tbsp Marsala wine (no other will do)

Put the butter and oil in a frying pan, over moderate heat. Add the garlic, and the prawns sautéing for three minutes. Turn the prawns over. Remove the garlic. Sprinkle on the salt and onion powder. Add the parsley, tarragon leaves, and wine. Reduce heat to low, cover and continue cooking for three more minutes.

Don't cook these until all else is set for dinner and your plates are ready with the other food. A baked potato is a good choice because it will stay hot.

Hotel Ione Scrapbook

The Hotel in 1930

The Hotel Café in 1977

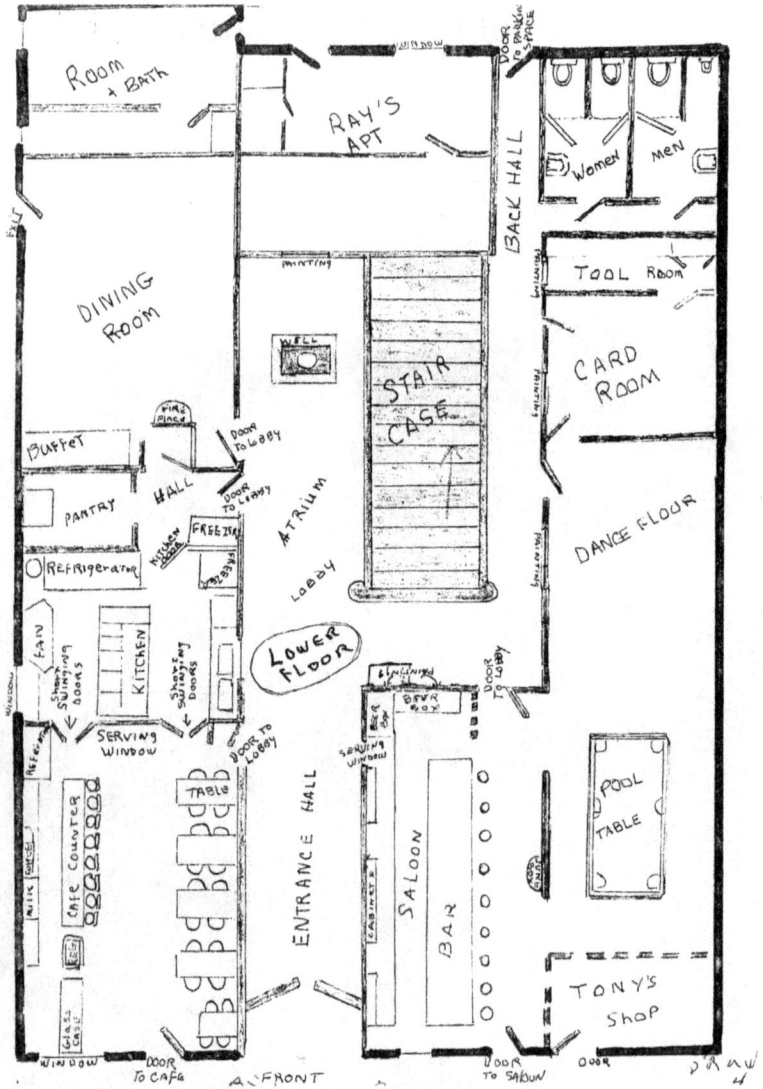

The Floor of the Hotel

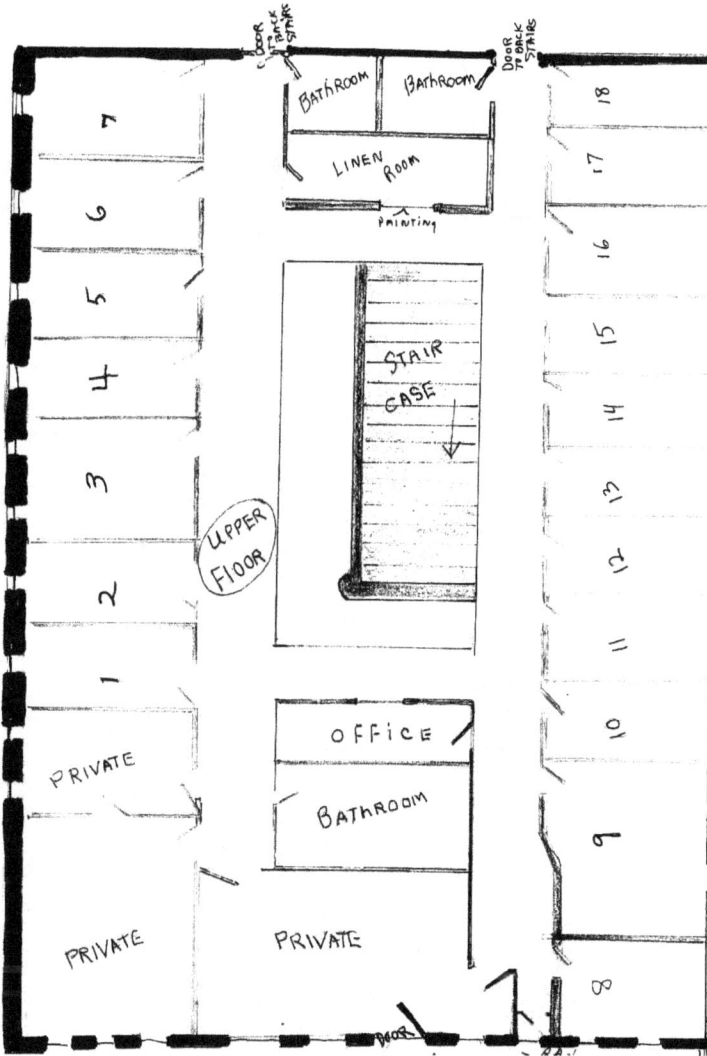

The Second Floor of the Hotel

HOTEL IONE
LUNCH

BURGER FOR LUNCH= (CHEESE) FRIES 1.90

DELUXE·BURGER·(CHEESE) SALAD and FRIES 2.45

PATTY MELT·BURGER= GRILLED ONIONS,CHEESE,ON RYE BREAD : FRIES 2.75

BIG CHILI BURGER CHOPPED CHEESE +ONIONS : FRIES 2.60

"GLOW BURGER", CHEESE + BACON GRILLED ONION : FRIES 2.65

HAMBURGER WITH CHIPS 1.30

FRENCH DIP : ROLL FILLED WITH BEEF SERVED WITH A·JU SAUCE +FRIES 2.85

LO·CAL PLATE= BURGER PATTY·COTTAGE CHEESE +FRUIT 2.05

HOT BEEF SANDWICH= MASHED POTATOES, LOTS OF GRAVY 3.10

STEAK SANDWICH : FRENCH ROLL, SALAD OR FRIES 4.50

CLUB HOUSE SANDWICH : TURKEY·HAM·OR BEEF·CHEESE·POTATO SALAD 380

GRILLED HAM and CHEESE. POTATO SALAD 2.85

B·L·T· BACON·LETTUCE·TOMATO WITH POTATO SALAD 2.25

GRILLED CHEESE· WITH CHIPS 1.55   COLD HAM·CHIPS 250

COLD BEEF·WITH CHIPS 2.25   COLD CHEESE·WITH CHIPS 1.55

COLD TURKEY·WITH CHIPS 205   TUNA FISH SANWICH·WITH CHIPS 205

SALADS. WE MAKE OUR OWN SALAD DRESSINGS : BLUE CHEESE=
THOUSAND ISLAND, FRENCH. + VINEGAR + OIL.

CHEF=HAM·CHEESE·TOMATO·CHOICE OF DRESSING 3320 HALF 1.65
·TUNA·CHEESE·TOMATO·CHOICE OF DRESSING   CHEF

FRUIT SALAD=MIXED FRUIT (CANNED) WITH COTTAGE CHEESE 2.25

DINNER SALAD= TOSSED GREEN. TOMATO·CROUTONS CHOICE OF DRESSING .85

MILK SHAKES .90   HOME MADE SOUPS
MALTS .95   CUP .50 BOWL 1.00
FLOATS ·70
SOFT DRINKS .40   HOMEMADE CHILI
ICED TEA .35   CUP .65 BOWL 1.30
MILK .50 SMALL .40
BEER : CAN 75 DRAFT MUG .50
WINE = GLASS 75 ½ LITRE 225 FULL LITRE 4.00

SIDE ORDERS
FRENCH FRIES 60   HOMEMADE PIES :
POTATO SALAD 60   +BREAD PUDDING WITH
MASHED POTATOS +GRAVY 60   RUM SAUCE.
COTTAGE CHEESE 60   " SEE OUR LETTER BOARD"

Hotel Ione Lunch Menu

218

DINNER

VEAL CUTLET - BREADED, GRILLED - WITH COUNTRY GRAVY _3.95_

LIVER + ONIONS FRIED WITH BACON _3.30_

CHICKEN FRIED STEAK: BREADED, GRILLED, WITH BROWN GRAVY _4.10_

NEW YORK STEAK: CHAR BROILED _6.40_

GROUND BEEF STEAK: CHAR BROILED _3.55_

SLICED TURKEY DINNER _3.95_

FRIED CHICKEN (DEEP FRIED) _4.35_

ROAST BEEF DINNER (TWO SLICES) _4.65_

FILLET OF SOLE (BREADED) GRILLED: LEMON + TARTER SAUCE _4.15_

SEA FOOD PLATTER (PRAWNS + CLAM STRIPS) DEEP FRIED _4.35_

ALL ENTREES INCLUDE: SOUP OR SALAD. CHOICE OF DRESSING
"BLUE CHEESE - THOUSAND ISLE - FRENCH = OIL + VINEGAR"
FRENCH FRIES OR REAL MASHED POTATOES + HOME MADE GRAVY + FR. BREAD.

Hotel Ione Dinner Menu

The Bottom of the Stairs, Pre-Renovations

The Bottom of the Stairs, Post-Renovations

Hotel Ione Dining Room Pre-Renovations

Hotel Ione Dining Room Post-Renovations

The Hotel Ione Staircase

The Well beside the Stairs, with Wheel, Bucket and Plants

The Hotel Ione Lobby

Renovations to the Dining Room – making a door from a window.

The top of the stairs – a painting was soon put over the window with a unicorn in a poppy field, painted by Cedora Scheiblich.

HOTEL · DINING ROOM · LUNCH ROOM · SALOON

BILL & MILLY JONES

PHONE
(209) 274-9945

41 MAIN ST.
IONE, CALIF. 95640

Hotel Ione Business Card

225

www.ingramcontent.com/pod-product-compliance
Lightning Source LLC
Chambersburg PA
CBHW052037090426
42739CB00010B/1945